Educating Children and Young People with Fetal Alcohol Spectrum Disorders

Constructing personalised pathways to learning

Carolyn Blackburn, Barry Carpenter, and Jo Egerton

 Routledge
Taylor & Francis Group

LONDON AND NEW YORK

First published 2012
by Routledge
2 Park Square, Milton Park, Abingdon, Oxon OX14 4RN

Simultaneously published in the USA and Canada
by Routledge
711 Third Avenue, New York, NY 10017

Routledge is an imprint of the Taylor & Francis Group, an informa business

British Library Cataloguing in Publication Data
A catalogue record for this book is available from the British Library

Library of Congress Cataloging in Publication Data
Blackburn, Carolyn, 1963–
Educating children and young people with fetal alcohol spectrum disorders : constructing personalised pathways to learning / Carolyn Blackburn, Barry Carpenter, Jo Egerton.
p. cm.
1. Learning disabled children–Education. 2. Fetal alcohol syndrome. 3. Individualized instruction. 4. Neurosciences. I. Carpenter, Barry. II. Egerton, Jo. III. Title.
LC4704.B56 2013
371.9–dc23
2011048436

ISBN: 978-0-415-67019-7 (hbk)
ISBN: 978-0-415-67020-3 (pbk)
ISBN: 978-0-203-11741-5 (ebk)

Typeset in Bembo by Prepress Projects Ltd, Perth, UK

Educating Children and Young People with Fetal Alcohol Spectrum Disorders

The range of learning difficulties associated with children who have fetal alcohol spectrum disorders (FASDs) has been highlighted as an emerging but little understood area of Special Educational Needs.

This engaging, timely, and highly practical book will raise awareness about FASDs and their associated difficulties across the entire education workforce. It provides a range of specialist, tried-and-tested practical teaching and learning strategies from which teachers and support staff may construct personalised learning plans for students with FASDs, and will help improve outcomes for all their children. It also:

- explains the impact that FASDs can have on a child's brain;
- discusses the overlapping and co-existing disorders, such as ADHD and autism spectrum disorders;
- shows how to support and empower teachers;
- provides ready-to-use teaching resources and strategies that can be used directly in the classroom.

Informed by the very latest research and written by leading experts in the field, *Educating Children and Young People with Fetal Alcohol Spectrum Disorders* will prove invaluable for experienced teachers and teaching assistants who are engaging in Continuing Professional Development, as well as newly qualified and training Initial Teacher Training students.

Carolyn Blackburn is an educational researcher and early years adviser currently based at Birmingham City University.

Barry Carpenter OBE was Director of the DfE Project on Children with Complex Learning Difficulties and Disabilities. He holds the iNet International Chair for Special and Inclusive Education, as well as Honorary Professorships at the Universities of Worcester and Limerick.

Jo Egerton is Research Project Co-ordinator for The Schools Network, and works on The Schools Network Research Charter Mark, supporting schools engaged in research.

Contents

Figures

Tables

Contributors

Carolyn Blackburn is an educational researcher and adviser. She was the project lead for the Fetal Alcohol Syndrome in Education (FAS-eD) Project as well as a project investigating Early Years Practitioner knowledge of fetal alcohol spectrum disorders. Carolyn has worked in childcare and education for 12 years as a researcher, adviser, early years manager, family support worker (early childhood intervention), development worker, early years tutor, and inclusion support worker. She is currently investigating the diverse communication needs of young children in the foundation stage at Birmingham City University. Carolyn has presented at conferences in the UK and Europe in relation to FASD, and co-authored articles for peer-reviewed journals with Barry and Jo.

Barry Carpenter was Director of the DfE-funded Project on Children with Complex Learning Difficulties and Disabilities, and of the TDA Project on Training for teachers of children with SLD, PMLD, and CLDD. He holds the iNet International Chair for Special and Inclusive Education as well as Honorary Professorships at the Universities of Worcester and Limerick. His postdoctoral research, at the University of Oxford, was in the education of children with fetal alcohol spectrum disorders. In a career spanning 30 years Barry has held the leadership positions of Headteacher, Principal, Academic Director, Inspector of Schools, and Director of the Centre for Special Education at Westminster College, Oxford. He has published widely on issues in the field of Special Education. He lectures nationally and internationally.

Jo Egerton is a Research Project Co-ordinator for The Schools Network, and worked on the DfE-funded Complex Learning Difficulties and Disabilities Research Project. She had a consultative role in the NOFAS-UK supported FAS-eD project for children with fetal alcohol spectrum disorders. She has worked in the field of special educational needs for 14 years in residential care, education, and research for students with severe and complex learning difficulties, and is currently working on The Schools Network's Research Charter Mark Award supporting schools engaged in research. Her previous co-edited books include *New Horizons in Special Education and Early Childhood Intervention* (with Barry Carpenter), and *Moving with Research* (with Elizabeth Marsden).

Foreword

It has been said by many great people throughout history, including Winston Churchill and Mahatma Ghandi, that a society can be judged by how it treats its most vulnerable groups. Yet, for a condition in which the immediate recognition of the disorder is not particularly easy, the challenge first to identify them and second to understand how best to help is a challenge.

Fetal alcohol spectrum disorders are a range of disorders, originally identified and labelled in 1973, that are caused when a pregnant woman consumes alcohol. The alcohol affects the developing fetus as a teratogen. However, because the body develops at different stages during the pregnancy, the timing of the alcohol consumption will affect which part of the body is damaged. Thus it is only a minority of affected individuals who have characteristic facial features. Considering that the most accepted part of the wider spectrum of conditions, fetal alcohol syndrome, is diagnosed primarily by the facial features, this means that the majority of those affected by prenatal alcohol exposure are not recognised.

Whereas the face is damaged at a discrete stage at the beginning of the pregnancy, the brain can be damaged throughout pregnancy. It begins to develop in the second or third week of pregnancy and continues to develop throughout. The timing of the alcohol consumption will, to some extent, define what an individual can and cannot do and which part of the brain is damaged. In the first trimester the basic structure forms. In the second and especially the third trimesters the brain expands rapidly and the different connections in the brain are formed. To interfere with this affects how information is processed and how learning occurs. This damage varies between individuals, but remains, to date, permanent. All this in someone who does not necessarily look any different from you or me.

Returning again to the idea that a society is judged by its ability to support those most vulnerable, it is therefore required to support those with visible and invisible disabilities. Unfortunately society does not always reflect this. The people with invisible disabilities are ones who are missed and their difficulties mislabelled. Studies by the Prison Reform Trust suggest that in some cases up to a third of those people in prison for low-level offences may have unrecognised cognition problems. FASDs are one group of disorders that will account for that population.

The level of knowledge about these disorders remains poor internationally. The UK is no different. The public and professionals remain groups who superficially seem to have heard about the disorder but know little more. As emerging research continues to suggest that this is the case, the worry is how we can make a change.

Those affected remain a group that are vulnerable and in need of support and help. Education is, for the majority, the first and main way that they can be helped. That education needs to be targeted to the level and needs of that individual group. For example, the range of needs of a condition such as those with non-complex attention deficit hyperactivity disorder (ADHD) will differ from the educational needs of people with a more complex form of ADHD. Given this, it becomes increasingly important to target the educational needs of specific groups. Although it is possible to begin from what is already known, modification and targeting of the strategies are vital.

For example, autistic spectrum disorders (ASDs) are a group of conditions with many causes. The association between prenatal alcohol and ASDs is increasingly being seen (Mukherjee *et al.*, 2011). Although that does not mean that ASDs are caused primarily by prenatal alcohol, as genetic conditions make up the majority of cases of ASDs, many more cases of ASDs are being linked to environmental causes such as alcohol. The type and presentation of ASDs, though, will differ. Thus, the starting point for the education of those children and young people who have ASDs most likely caused by prenatal alcohol, or where there has been a strong association with prenatal alcohol exposure, may well be what is already known about effective educational strategies for children with ASDs. It is only by modification of the pre-existing strategies, however, that the needs of this subgroup and their specific learning needs will be addressed. It may well be that, ultimately, new strategies that are unique to this group will have to be created.

The strategies and information presented in this book have begun the process of adapting what is known from other learning disability areas and from other parts of the world to children and young people with FASDs. Overall, once the recognition of this disorder improves, once the knowledge of professionals and of the public increases, and the recommendations in this book are adopted, it may be possible that the outcomes for this and other largely invisible groups will begin to improve. Only then can society claim to support the vulnerable.

Raja A.S. Mukherjee, Lead Clinician, FASD Specialist Behaviour Clinic,
Surrey and Borders Partnership NHS Foundation Trust

Reference

Mukherjee, R.A.S., Layton, M., Yacoub, E., and Turk, J. (2011) 'Autism and autistic traits in people exposed to heavy prenatal alcohol: data from a clinical series of 21 individuals and nested case control study', *Advances in Mental Health and Intellectual Disabilities*, 5 (1): 42–49.

Acknowledgements

The contents of this book owe much of their origin to an educational research project (FAS-eD Project) undertaken by NOFAS-UK (www.nofas-uk.org) in which the authors were involved. Barry Carpenter was the Research Director, Jo Egerton the Research Associate, and Carolyn Blackburn the Project Researcher.

The FAS-eD project would not have been possible without the children and young people, families, and educators who participated, and this book is dedicated to them, and all individuals affected by prenatal alcohol exposure. The authors are grateful to Professor Hilary Constable, Susan Fleisher, and Dr Raja Mukherjee for their support and contribution to the project.

The book also draws on the research findings from the Complex Learning Difficulties and Disabilities Project (www.ssatrust.org.uk), for which Barry was the Research Director, Jo the Research Co-ordinator, and Carolyn an adviser and researcher for the mainstream/early years phase of the project.

Other organisations providing support for families and advocacy for individuals affected by FASDs in the UK are FAS Aware UK (www.fasaware.co.uk) and the FASD Trust (www.fasdtrust.co.uk).

Chapter 1

Introduction

Fetal alcohol spectrum disorders (FASDs) comprise a broad spectrum of completely preventable intellectual and developmental deficits in individuals resulting from maternal alcohol consumption during pregnancy. FASDs include a range of physical and intellectual disabilities (BMA, 2007). Possible physical disabilities include facial differences, growth deficiencies, major organ damage, and skeletal damage, as well as hearing and vision impairments. Damage to the brain (central nervous system damage) results in developmental disabilities, which can include general learning difficulties, communication delays/disorders, and behavioural, social and emotional, and sensory difficulties (Jones and Smith, 1973; Stratton *et al.*, 1996; Matson and Riley, 1997). These difficulties are summarised by the honesty of CJ, a young adult with an FASD:

> I have trouble with some stuff, like maths, spelling, left and right and memory. I try to get good grades so that I can be like smart people, but when I get good grades, they [other young adults] call me a cheater, so I can't win. I want to be like other adults but I can't be like other adults because I can't take the bus and I don't want to drive and I get worried a lot . . . more than other people . . . it's frustrating.
>
> (NOFAS-UK, 2010a)

Children and young people (CYP) with FASDs have particular strengths of a practical nature, but the difficulties described above persist throughout life (BMA, 2007) and impact on daily living skills, peer and family relationships, and employment prospects (Blackburn, 2010), and require a particular learning environment and teaching approach. In a typical classroom, CYP with FASDs present educators with the following challenges: hyperactivity; short attention span; erratic mood swings; poor memory; lack of social skills; auditory/vocal processing; visual sequencing; sensory integration difficulties (particularly lack of co-ordination); poor retention of task instruction; and numeracy/mathematical difficulties (Carpenter, 2011).

Fetal alcohol spectrum disorders now account for the largest group of CYP presenting with non-genetic learning difficulties/disabilities (Abel and Sokol, 1987, cited in BMA, 2007, p. 2).

The difficulties that CYP with FASDs face in the classroom epitomise that much-used phrase 'complex needs' (Dittrich and Tutt, 2008; Carpenter, 2011). FASDs often co-exist with other conditions such as attention deficit hyperactivity disorder (ADHD), autistic spectrum disorders (ASDs), and oppositional defiant disorder (ODD) and may be compounded by attachment difficulties and sensory processing difficulties (Blackburn, 2010; Carpenter, 2011).

Where are the children with fetal alcohol spectrum disorders in our schools?

Children and young people with FASDs may account for as many as 1 in 100 children (Autti-Ramo, 2002), with difficulties ranging from mild to profound (Carpenter *et al.*, 2011), including physical, learning, and behavioural difficulties and disabilities. This means that some CYP with FASDs will have needs that are evident at birth and easily diagnosed, and will be recognisable by educators as in need of support. However, other CYP with FASDs will have hidden needs (Blackburn, 2010; Carpenter, 2011), which make the educator's role more challenging. In addition, 'underdiagnosis' (sometimes referred to as misdiagnosis; see Carpenter, 2011, and Chapters 2 and 5 of this book), when conditions such as ASD or ADHD are diagnosed instead of FASDs, can mean that CYP are presented with a curriculum which is only partially suitable for their needs (see Blackburn, 2010). Do you have CYP with FASDs in your classroom?

If only I'd known . . .

Educators would do things differently if only they knew. Egerton (2009) points out that CYP with FASDs have no control over behaviours which parents and educators may find unacceptable or undesirable, for example not following instructions, forgetting rules, not relating to others appropriately, disrupting others, displaying emotional outbursts, and inappropriate interactions with other children and adults.

Children and young people affected by FASDs can also face misunderstanding about the often hidden cause of their very challenging learning behaviours, particularly where there are no obvious physical differences, as is most often the case.

The unusual style of learning and extreme challenging behaviour of CYP affected is out of the experience of many educators and, as there has been a significant shortfall in guidance for educators on how to teach children with FASDs in the UK, teachers find themselves 'pedagogically bereft' (Carpenter, 2011).

Importance of recognising learners with fetal alcohol spectrum disorders and addressing their needs

The importance of accurate and early diagnosis of FASDs has been recognised by many writers including parents (Fleisher, 2007, cited in BMA, 2007) and researchers (Streissguth and Kanter, 1997; Streissguth *et al.*, 2004; Egerton, 2009; Blackburn, 2010; Carpenter, 2011).

As Carpenter (2011) points out, we have only to listen to the profound words of Elizabeth Russell, a mother of two sons with FASDs, to recognise that people wish that they had been given appropriate warnings upon which they could have based effective personal choices – not only for themselves, but also for their offspring:

> If my son, Mick's, paediatrician had enquired about my alcohol intake when he diagnosed Mick at six months of age as 'possibly retarded', Seth (my other son) would not now have Fetal Alcohol Syndrome. We would have two relatively healthy children in whose future was woven the thread of peace and contentment, not fear and apprehension, and I would never again have to look at my son's terrified eyes hiding behind a make-believe smile.
>
> (Russell, 2011, cited in Carpenter, 2011, p. 6)

Early diagnosis not only supports CYP affected by FASDs within the family context, but can have the benefit of preventing FASDs in those yet to be born.

The often complex family structure for CYP with FASDs, combined with lack of knowledge about FASDs amongst local authorities and social and health services, can imply that parents and carers have difficulty accessing effective and appropriate support to meet the diverse and changing needs of their son/daughter with an FASD.

The importance of valuing the contribution of 'key family members', including those related by social ties as well as blood ties (Carpenter, 2010, p. 4), in order to be 'responsive to the daily context the family finds themselves in' (ibid.) is crucial if educational settings are to take their responsibilities to CYP and families seriously, particularly where the family structure may change often, as can be the case for children with FASDs. Carpenter and colleagues (2011, p. 18) remind us of the rights of every child to be included as a learner within the curriculum, however great their degree of disability or learning difficulty. Article 29 of the United Nations Convention on the Rights of the Child recognises society's responsibility to develop children's personality, talents, and mental and physical abilities to their fullest potential through education (United Nations, 1989).

Hope for children and families affected by fetal alcohol spectrum disorders

Recognition of the need to understand the needs of CYP and families affected by FASDs is increasing. In terms of education, until recently, there was no direct guidance from any government agency in the UK to educators on how to teach CYP with FASDs. However, in October 2010, NOFAS-UK (www.nofas-uk.org) published a significant report offering guidance to teachers in all age phases. In August 2011, the Specialist Schools and Academies Trust (now called The Schools Network) published a report relating to CYP with complex learning difficulties and disabilities (CLDD), of which FASDs were a significant aspect (Carpenter et al., 2011).

The three major parent-led organisations in the UK, NOFAS-UK (www.nofas-uk.org), the

FASD Trust (www.fasdtrust.co.uk), and FAS Aware (www.fasaware.co.uk), provide guidance and support for parents. The European Birth Mother Support Network (www.eurobmsn.org/), launched in 2010, is a network of women who drank alcohol during pregnancy and may have CYP with FASDs. The network is a place where mothers can share their experience and support each other.

In terms of medical and health-related initiatives, the World Health Organization adopted a global strategy to reduce harmful use of alcohol at the 63rd World Health Assembly, May 2010. Item 21c of the section 'Policy Options and Interventions' states goals of 'improving capacity for prevention of, identification of, and interventions for individuals and families living with fetal alcohol syndrome and a spectrum of associated disorders' (World Health Organization, 2010, p. 12).

In the UK, the first FASD clinic, run by Dr Raja Mukherjee (www.sabp.nhs.uk/services/specialist/fetal-alcohol-spectrum-disorder-fasd-clinic), offers specialist advice on the diagnosis of FASDs. It carries out detailed assessments of young children's speech, language, and brain functions relative to their age. These assessments include photographic analysis of the child's facial features to complete the diagnosis.

The 'Alcohol in Pregnancy – Training for Midwives Project' is an initiative of NOFAS-UK (2010a) designed to provide useful positive health information about the consumption of alcohol in pregnancy to midwives, who play an important role and can help prevent FASDs. The project has been reviewed by the Royal College of Midwives and the International FASD Medical Advisory Panel.

The advice to women relating to alcohol consumption during pregnancy remains controversial. The 2008 update to the NICE (National Institute for Health and Clinical Excellence) guidelines advised women to refrain from alcohol consumption during the first trimester and limit their consumption to one or two UK units per week thereafter (Royal College of Obstetricians and Gynaecologists, 2008, p. 16). NOFAS-UK through its Baby Bundle project advises 'no alcohol consumption during pregnancy', a view echoed internationally by the eminent medical researcher, and Professor of Paediatrics at the University of Washington, Dr Sterling Clarren (NOFAS-UK, 2010b). For a full discussion of the range of advice given to women on these issues see BMA (2007).

In terms of social care, The Adolescent and Children's Trust (TACT) is the UK's largest charity and voluntary agency providing fostering and adoption services (www.tactcare.org.uk).

In some countries, such as Canada and the USA, there is extensive guidance and a well-developed system of provision for these children. This depth and extent of provision is needed in the UK with some urgency.

About this book

This book aims to inform educators and the range of multi-disciplinary professionals who support CYP in educational settings about the implications of FASDs on:

- learning and development;
- attachment with others;
- family life;
- life outcomes;
- society.

It will also be useful to those working in social care, fostering and adoption services, respite care, and extended service settings such as short-break provision and holiday provision.

The chapters in this book can be read and used and referred to in any order; however, in order to use the teaching and learning strategies most effectively, the background and complementary information contained in the preceding chapters will be most usefully read first.

Chapter 2 looks at the history and effects of alcohol use on the developing baby in the womb. It also discusses how FASDs are identified and the likely numbers of affected CYP.

Chapters 3 and 4 discuss the impact of FASDs on learning and development, including an overview of some of the compounding factors such as attachment difficulties, sensory processing difficulties, and poor mental health. Chapter 4 provides some evidence-based teaching and learning strategies for educators and other professionals to use when designing appropriate curricula for CYP. Case studies provide an insight into how individual CYP have been supported in educational settings in the UK in various aspects of their learning and development.

Chapter 5 looks at the complex pattern of learning presented by children with FASDs. It defines their learning behaviour in the context of the overarching diagnosis of CLDD. Through a profile of the uneven and inconsistent patterns of learning in children with FASDs, the chapter recommends a new pedagogical framework in which to plan effective learning experiences. These are built on the tenet of 'engagement'. A case study details how the use of the 'engagement profile and scale' can illuminate pathways to progress for a child with an FASD.

Chapter 6 outlines the complex family dynamics, and provides educators and professionals with a platform for understanding the nature of difficulties faced by families affected by FASDs. Birth and adoptive families are discussed and the importance of early attachment is highlighted in order for educators to understand the underlying nature of difficulties faced by CYP with FASDs in their early development.

Chapter 7 concludes the text by suggesting possible curriculum approaches to support CYP with FASDs, putting families at the centre of the support package offered in order to enable those affected to reach optimal progress and long-term well being.

References

Autti-Rämö, I. (2002) 'Foetal Alcohol Syndrome: a multifaceted condition', *Developmental Medicine and Child Neurology*, 44: 141–144.

Blackburn, C. (2010) *Facing the Challenge and Shaping the Future for Primary and Secondary Aged Students with Foetal Alcohol Spectrum Disorders* (FAS-eD Project). London: National Organisation on Fetal Alcohol Syndrome (UK). Online at: www.nofas-uk.org, accessed 27 July 2011.

BMA (British Medical Association) (2007) *Foetal Alcohol Spectrum Disorders: A Guide for Healthcare Professionals*. London: British Medical Association.

Carpenter, B. (2010) *Complex Needs Series No. 6: The Family Context, Community and Society*. London: Specialist Schools and Academies Trust.

Carpenter, B. (2011) 'Pedagogically bereft! Improving learning outcomes for children with Foetal Alcohol Spectrum Disorders', *British Journal of Special Education*, 38 (1): 37–43.

Carpenter, B., Egerton, J., Brooks, T., Cockbill, B., Fotheringham, J., and Rawson, H. (2011) *The Complex Learning Difficulties and Disabilities Research Project: Developing Meaningful Pathways to Personalised Learning Final Report*. London: Specialist Schools and Academies Trust (SSAT).

Dittrich, W.H. and Tutt, R. (2008) *Educating Children with Complex Conditions: Understanding Overlapping and Co-existing Developmental Disorders*. London: Sage Publications.

Egerton, J. (2009) *Foetal Alcohol Spectrum Disorder Information Sheets*. Worcester: Sunfield Research Institute/Worcestershire County Council.

Jones, K.L. and Smith, D.W. (1973) 'Recognition of the fetal alcohol syndrome in early infancy', *Lancet*, 2 (7836): 999–1001.

Mattson, S.N. and Riley, E.P. (1997) 'Neurobehavioural and neuroanatomical effects of heavy prenatal exposure to alcohol', in Streissguth, A. and Kanter, J. (eds) *The Challenges of Fetal Alcohol Symdrome Overcoming Secondary Disabilities*. Seattle: University of Washington Press, pp. 3–14.

NOFAS-UK (2010a) *A Child for Life: A Film on Families Coping with Children with Foetal Alcohol Spectrum Disorder*. London: NOFAS-UK.

NOFAS-UK (2010b) *Alcohol in Pregnancy: Information for Midwives*. London: NOFAS-UK.

Royal College of Obstetricians and Gynaecologists (2008) *Antenatal Care Routine Care for the Healthy Pregnant Woman*. Commissioned by the National Institute for Health and Clinical Excellence. London: RCOG.

Stratton, K., Howe, C., and Battaglia, F. (eds) (1996) *Fetal Alcohol Syndrome: Diagnosis, Epidemiology, Prevention and Treatment*. Washington, DC: National Academy Press.

Streissguth, A. and Kanter, J. (eds) (1997) *The Challenges of Fetal Alcohol Syndrome: Overcoming Secondary Disabilities*. Seattle: University of Washington Press.

Streissguth, A.P., Bookstein, F., Barr, H., Sampson, P.D., O'Malley, K. and Young, J.K. (2004) 'Risk factors for adverse life outcomes in fetal alcohol syndrome and fetal alcohol effects', *Journal of Developmental and Behavioural Pediatrics*, 24: 228–238.

United Nations (1989) *Conventions on the Right of the Child, Article 29*. Office of the United Nations High Commissioner for Human Rights. Online at: www2.ohchr.org/english/law/crc.htm#art29, accessed 14 January 2012.

World Health Organization (2010) *Global Strategy to Reduce the Harmful Use of Alcohol*. Geneva: WHO. Online at: www.who.int/substance_abuse/activities/gsrhua/en/index.html, accessed 13 September 2011.

Chapter 2

Fetal alcohol spectrum disorders

History, diagnosis, causes, and prevalence

This chapter looks at the history and effects of alcohol use on the developing baby in the womb. It also discusses how fetal alcohol spectrum disorders (FASDs) are identified and the likely numbers of affected children and young people (CYP).

While reading, it is important to keep in mind that birth mothers of CYP with FASDs have often been unaware of the damage they were causing to their baby by drinking during pregnancy. More UK research is needed in this area, but MacKinnion (Mukherjee *et al.*, 2006) found that among a group of American teenagers, although 97 per cent realised that alcohol affected the unborn baby, 48 per cent thought this meant that the baby was addicted to alcohol and over 50 per cent thought any damage could be cured. Such beliefs were also held by UK teenagers interviewed for BBC One's *Inside Out* (BBC One, 2009). In addition, some mothers have used alcohol to find relief from troubled and disrupting life experiences, for example abuse and psychiatric problems (Astley *et al.*, 2000a,b; Riley, 2011). It needs an enormous amount of strength to overcome difficulties and disadvantages, which professionals can only guess at, to take a supporting and determining role in their child's education and future.

How alcohol affects the developing baby

As stated earlier, alcohol is a 'teratogen': a substance which can potentially cause a baby in the womb to develop abnormally (West and Blake, 2005). Alcohol is one teratogen amongst many – for example, environmental contaminants, such as lead and mercury; other recreational drugs, such as tobacco, cocaine, methamphetamines, marijuana, and opiates (Lebel *et al.*, 2011) – which are often used in combination. However, the US Institute of Medicine (2006) stated:

> Of all the substances of abuse . . . alcohol produces by far the most serious neurobehavioural effects in the fetus.

Approximately one in ten women continues to drink while pregnant. When a pregnant woman drinks alcohol, it is quickly absorbed into her body and, within 10 to 15 minutes, crosses the placenta by diffusion from the mother's to the baby's blood. The developing baby is exposed to the same blood alcohol levels as the mother (Luu, 2010; Substance Abuse and Mental Health Services Administration, 2010), but, because of developmental immaturity, is largely dependent on the mother's liver to break down the alcohol. For the mother, approximately one unit of alcohol is metabolised per hour (British Liver Trust, 2010) but the process of alcohol breakdown is much slower in the fetus. Alcohol is also absorbed into the amniotic fluid surrounding the baby. The rate at which alcohol is eliminated from amniotic fluid is about half that for blood, and so it acts as a reservoir for alcohol, increasing the length of time the baby is exposed (Luu, 2010; Vaux, 2010).

Alcohol alters fetal development. It can cause fetal cell death, and disrupt the way cells specialise, grow, and migrate to create different parts of the developing baby, most significantly the neurons in the brain. It can reduce the flow of blood to the fetal brain. It changes the way the mother metabolises food, and decreases the essential enzymes and nutrients reaching the baby across the placenta. Therefore alcohol both permanently changes how a baby is formed and deprives it of the food needed for healthy development. Therefore, at birth, such infants can be malnourished, and there is also evidence that they may suffer from low blood oxygen levels (Weinberg, 2009; Vaux, 2010; Lebel *et al.*, 2011).

Prenatal alcohol exposure and its historic impact

The accepted modern theory of how a mother's alcohol consumption affects the unborn child began in France with initial work by Rouquette (1957), Heuyer and colleagues (1957), and Christiaens and colleagues (1960), who noted neurological disorders and delayed growth and development of babies born to alcoholic mothers. Lemoine (1968) identified a characteristic pattern of abnormalities, including delayed growth, microcephaly (small head), specific facial differences, organ/skeletal malformations, gross and fine motor difficulties, and behavioural issues (Kulaga, 2009), which he called 'alcoholic embryopathy' (NOFAS-UK, 2010). In the USA, Jones and Smith (1973), working without knowledge of Lemoine's research, noted a similar pattern, and coined the term 'fetal alcohol syndrome'. They were the first to describe in detail a consistent characteristic pattern of impairments associated with prenatal alcohol exposure, and to propose diagnostic criteria (Hoyme *et al.*, 2005).

During the 1970s, there was scepticism about whether the effects described above were caused by alcohol. Other causes such as malnutrition, liver disease, and other drugs were suggested (West and Blake, 2005; Weinberg, 2009). People questioned why, as alcohol had been drunk for centuries, the link had not been made before. This triggered a search for historical evidence relating to alcohol use in pregnancy.

It was discovered that influential thinkers through history had identified alcohol as a threat to the health of the unborn child, and identified a range of causes and outcomes. For example, Plato (427–347 BC) in his *Laws* (University of Chicago, 2009) warned of the consequences for a baby conceived when the father was 'steeped in wine'. In 1623, the philosopher Francis Bacon noted in his book *Sylva Sylvarum* that 'the diet of women with child doth work much upon the infant'. He advised that a mother 'endangereth the child to become lunatic, or of imperfect memory' by indulging in actions which 'send or draw vapours to the head'. His list of actions included the following when done to excess: fasting, intake of wine or strong drink, but also eating of onions or beans and 'musing' (Spedding et al., 1857–1859). However, claims for historic recognition of prenatal alcohol effects on CYP should be approached with caution. Abel (1997, 1999a,b, 2001) has written about the unreliability of examples taken out of context, and these articles should be read alongside other accounts. Nevertheless, the excessive drinking of alcohol has been associated with poor birth outcomes over centuries, even if the exact causes were mistaken or misattributed.

The anecdotal outcomes noted as a result of parental heavy drinking in early writings can be matched with some of the features associated with fetal alcohol syndrome recognised by modern science. A range of historic quotations (Plant, 1985) appear to describe CYP who had impairments ('defective'), growth delay ('puny and emaciated'), and motor difficulties ('ungainly'), were irritable and failed to thrive ('weak, feeble and distempered'), and had learning difficulties ('beneath the standard of a rational human being').

In the late nineteenth century, the observations of effects of prenatal alcohol became more evidence-based and began to confirm earlier anecdotal evidence and dispel myths. In 1865, Lanceraux, a French doctor, described CYP born to mothers who drank alcohol habitually as having small heads and atypical facial features and suffering from nervousness and convulsions, and Dr William Sullivan, working in Liverpool in 1899, found that pregnancy outcomes among 120 alcoholic female prisoners, compared with 28 of their relatives, resulted in a 20 per cent higher infant mortality rate. He noted a pattern of birth defects, and also observed that babies born in prison, where their mothers had to stop drinking alcohol partway through pregnancy, tended to be healthier (Hoyme et al., 2005).

Early in the twentieth century, although some contrary evidence existed, most people believed that birth defects were inherited. Teratogens were recognised in the 1940s, but not defined until the 1960s after thalidomide, a morning sickness drug, had caused limb malformation among babies on a wide scale (West and Blake, 2005). Although an interest in prenatal alcohol-related outcomes for CYP waned during the first half of the twentieth century, the research of the 1950s, 1960s, and 1970s described above formed the basis of today's understanding of how prenatal alcohol affects the fetus.

Patterns of alcohol use

The severity and type of fetal damage caused by maternal alcohol use depend on a variety of factors including (Jonsson et al., 2009; Mattson and Riley, 2011; Morleo et al., 2011):

- level and duration of drinking;
- pattern of drinking;
- timing of alcohol consumption (i.e. stage of fetal development);
- blood alcohol level;

- genetic influences;
- maternal age and health – physiological effects;
- use of other teratogens;
- postnatal factors.

Level of drinking

Although widely referred to, there is no common definition of light, moderate, heavy, and binge drinking. Kelly and colleagues (2009), in a study of light drinking during pregnancy, used the following definitions:

- light – not more than one to two units per week or per occasion;
- moderate – not more than three to six units per week or three to five units per occasion;
- heavy/binge (heavy and episodic) – seven or more units per week or six or more units per occasion.

The severity of FASDs in CYP appears to relate to the amount of alcohol used by the mother in pregnancy (Public Health Agency of Canada, 2010). When fetal alcohol syndrome (FAS) was first named, it was taken to be caused by heavy drinking in certain minority populations. However, it is now widely accepted that the condition is found within the general population, and that moderate consumption can also give rise to FASD (Gray et al., 2009; May et al., 2011). A range of studies looking at the effects of moderate drinking during pregnancy on outcomes for CYP have associated it with poor growth, cognition, and behavioural outcomes, including attention and memory problems, hyperactivity, impulsivity, poor social and communication skills, psychiatric problems (including mood disorders), and alcohol and drug use (Jacobson et al., 2004; March of Dimes, 2008; Gray et al., 2009). There is also an ongoing debate about whether light drinking during pregnancy increases the risk of behaviour problems and cognitive deficits for CYP. Some studies have found no association (e.g. Kelly et al., 2009), whereas others have found the opposite (e.g. Mukherjee et al., 2005; O'Connor et al., 2006). However, researchers generally agree that it is not known how certain mothers and fetuses with particular genetic or metabolic profiles will be affected by alcohol even at low levels. This being the case, many on both sides of the debate conclude that the only safe course of action is not to drink alcohol during pregnancy.

The UK's directives on the use of alcohol in pregnancy come from the National Institute for Health and Clinical Excellence (NICE) and the UK's Chief Medical Officers. These are in agreement, and a directive from the latter states:

> As a general rule, pregnant women or women trying to conceive should avoid drinking alcohol. If they do choose to drink, to protect the baby they should not drink more than 1 to 2 units of alcohol once or twice a week and should not get drunk.

The agreed shortened form of this advice from the UK Chief Medical Officers is to 'Avoid alcohol while pregnant or trying to conceive' (Department of Health, 2009).

Pattern of drinking

The outcomes for the fetus become more serious with each alcohol exposure during pregnancy (Gibbard, 2009). Binge drinking is also associated with more harmful effects than the same amount of alcohol taken over a longer period (Maier and West, 2001). At any stage during pregnancy, if a mother reduces her alcohol intake or manages to stop drinking the outcomes are better for the fetus (Vaux, 2010).

Timing of alcohol use

There are poor outcomes for the fetus of prenatal alcohol exposure at any stage in pregnancy, but evidence suggests that the effects are different depending on the developmental stage of the fetus when alcohol is used. This is described in more detail below.

Blood alcohol level

At higher concentrations of alcohol in the blood, the harm done to the developing fetus is increased.

Genetic influence

The effects of prenatal alcohol exposure may be affected by the mother's and baby's genetic make-up – which can make drinking alcohol less desirable for the mother and/or can affect how quickly alcohol is eliminated from the mother's and baby's bodies (Gray et al., 2009).

Health and age of the mother

The damage to the developing baby in the womb is more likely to be severe if the mother is undernourished. Body fat reduces the impact of the alcohol on the fetus. Therefore, the lower the mother's body fat, the less protection is given to the baby (May, 2009). A mother's body fat is also lower with increased age, heightening the likelihood of serious outcomes in children born to older mothers.

Postnatal factors

The features of FASDs are complex. In addition to a CYP's genetic make-up, other influences such as environment bring about individualised FASD effects. A brain damaged by alcohol is vulnerable to negative influences, and, over the affected child's life, changes in these factors can impact positively or negatively (Mattson and Riley, 2011). Factors include environment (e.g. poverty), stress (e.g. abuse or neglect), family interactions and situation (e.g. socio-economic status; cultural influences), and level of continuing paediatric and health care (Gibbard, 2009; Jonsson et al., 2009; Coles, 2011).

The different ways alcohol may affect a baby

There is no period in pregnancy during which alcohol can be drunk without risk. The timing of fetal alcohol exposure results in different harms (Warren et al., 2011), and during the most sensitive periods of development it can result in major structural or functional impairments (US Department of Health and Human Services et al., 2008). The facial differences associated with FAS are thought to occur when significant alcohol is drunk during a specific development window in the first trimester (first three months) of pregnancy (Streissguth and O'Malley, 2000; Mattson and Riley, 2011). The heart and other organs, including the bones, are also at risk at this time. In the early weeks of pregnancy, and during the second trimester, the fetus has an increased risk of spontaneous abortion, and in the third trimester the effects of alcohol on the fetus include impaired height, weight, and brain development (Chudley et al., 2005). However, the fetal central nervous system (including eyes and ears) remains very vulnerable to the effects of alcohol throughout pregnancy (US Department of Health and Human Services et al., 2008; Mattson and Riley, 2011). Riley (2011) suggests that, early in pregnancy, alcohol might impact on the number of cells in brain structures (e.g. the corpus callosum, which connects the two brain hemispheres), whereas later it could affect the number of connections between brain cells or how quickly neurons can transmit nerve impulses. It might also cause cerebellum anomalies, thus affecting balance, attention, and classical conditioning (Figure 2.1).

Diagnosis

As the previous chapter has noted, 'fetal alcohol spectrum disorder (FASD)' is an umbrella term used to encompass the range of possible effects of prenatal exposure to alcohol (Bertrand et al., 2005; BMA, 2007), including FAS, partial fetal alcohol syndrome (pFAS), and alcohol-related effects or fetal alcohol effects (FAEs). FAEs include alcohol-related neurodevelopmental disorder (ARND) and alcohol-related birth defects (ARBDs). These effects may include physical, mental, behavioural, and/or learning disabilities with possible lifelong implications (Bertrand et al., 2005).

Only FAS can be formally diagnosed using the criteria within the *International Classification of Diseases (ICD-10-CM)* (World Health Organization, 2011). Although the related clinical conditions are recognised (Bertrand et al., 2005; Hoyme et al., 2005), there are currently no distinctive behavioural or neurobiological profiles associated with them (Gray and Mukherjee, 2007). The search for such a profile is one current focus of FASD research.

The easiest time to identify FAS is in early childhood when a child is aged between six

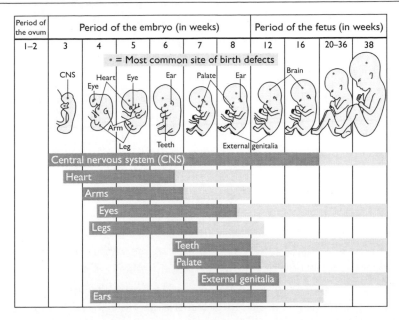

Figure 2.1 Vulnerability of the fetus to defects during different periods of development. The dark portion of the bars represents the most sensitive periods of development, during which teratogenic effects on the sites listed would result in major structural abnormalities in the child. The lighter portion of the bars represents periods of development during which physiological defects and minor structural abnormalities would occur. Source: adapted from National Organization on Fetal Alcohol Syndrome, 2004; adapted from Moore, 1993.

months and three years and facial and growth differences are most pronounced; as the young person grows older these physical distinctions gradually fade – unlike the impaired brain function and behavioural difficulties, which are lifelong (Chandrasena et al., 2009). For other fetal alcohol exposure conditions, the early school years, when the child is six or seven years old, may be better. At this time, children can take part in formal neurodevelopmental assessments which will pick up difficulties in key areas such as executive functioning (May, 2009).

Fetal alcohol syndrome

Fetal alcohol syndrome is the most identifiable of the FASDs and is the only one on the spectrum which can be diagnosed without knowing the mother's history of alcohol use during pregnancy. However, diagnosis is difficult even for medical practitioners. Although the process may be started by an informed family doctor, they would usually seek the involvement or advice of specialist clinicians (e.g. clinical psychologist, clinical geneticist/dysmorphologist, neurologist, developmental–behavioural paediatrician). These specialists have in-depth knowledge and understanding of dysmorphology, neurodevelopmental assessment, and the wide range of dysfunctions associated with prenatal alcohol exposure (Chudley *et al.*, 2005; Hoyme *et al.*, 2005; Gahagan *et al.*, 2006).

There are three key characteristics which can lead to diagnosis of FAS (Gray and Mukherjee, 2007; World Health Organization, 2011):

- facial differences – flattening of the mid-line groove between nose and mouth (philtrum), a thin upper lip (vermillion border), and narrowing of the opening between upper and lower eyelids (small palpebral fissures);
- delayed growth – below average height, weight, or both (below the tenth percentile);
- central nervous system (CNS) abnormalities – structural, neurological, functional or a combination. These may include microcephaly, learning disabilities, developmental delay, hyperactivity disorders, seizures and brain structure abnormalities – described in greater detail in Appendix A. In newborns, this may include excessive irritability, hyperactivity, seizures, or tremors.

Non-specialists should not guess at diagnosis based upon observed features. Although associated with FAS, particular features are also found in other conditions, for example in some rare chromosomal conditions (e.g. Williams syndrome, Cornelia de Lange syndrome, velo-cardiofacial syndrome and Noonan syndrome, among others) (Chudley et al., 2005; Hoyme et al., 2005). The FAS neurobehavioural characteristics are also found in conditions other than FASDs (Mattson and Riley, 2011). Importantly, diagnosis of FAS therefore also involves excluding other conditions (Hoyme et al., 2005; Andrew, 2009; Benz et al., 2009).

There are also common non-diagnostic differences in FAS including:

- other facial differences (due to bone structure abnormalities);
- organ and skeletal malformations;
- sensory impairments;
- muscle tone and co-ordination difficulties;
- otherwise unexplained behavioural and cognitive issues.

CYP with FASDs may have complex health issues. If this is the case, it is essential that they have regular medical check-ups to monitor physical difficulties.

A child who has been exposed to alcohol prenatally may have only some of the facial features of FAS. Where there is also evidence of at least one other associated characteristic – growth deficiency, neurodevelopmental abnormalities, or a complex pattern of behavioural or cognitive abnormalities which cannot be explained through family background or environment – the condition is known as partial FAS (pFAS) (Hoyme et al., 2005).

Whereas the FAS physical differences are the most noticeable, the effect of prenatal alcohol exposure on the brain – and the resulting cognitive and behavioural effects – has the greatest impact for CYP with FASDs (Riley et al., 2011). The damage is widespread, involving almost the whole brain, and affects not only CYP with the most severe dysmorphology, but also those with fewer cognitive and behavioural symptoms (Lebel et al., 2011).

Magnetic resonance imaging (MRI) has allowed brain research to become more sophisticated. Lebel and colleagues (2011) note that the most common MRI findings, in relation to prenatal alcohol exposure, are reduced brain volume and abnormalities of the corpus callosum.

Warren and colleagues (2011) describe how various MRI techniques and neurobehavioural research have revealed high sensitivities of certain brain regions to alcohol, including the frontal cortex, caudate, hippocampal formation, corpus callosum, and components of the cerebellum, including the anterior cerebellar vermis; damage to white matter tracts (i.e. nerve fibre bundles) may alter how the brain processes information; behavioural and cognitive difficulties have been linked with alterations in the functioning of certain CNS regions. Other imaging techniques have shown that alcohol exposure affects cerebral blood flow and brain signalling systems (Warren *et al.*, 2011).

In recent years, the diagnostic tools for FAS/FASDs have been refined to make them more clinically useful (Bertrand *et al.*, 2005; Hoyme *et al.*, 2005; West and Blake, 2005; Benz *et al.*, 2009). The original four-digit diagnostic code (or 'Washington criteria') is now in its third edition (Astley and Clarren, 2000; Astley, 2004), and the US Institute of Medicine's criteria were updated in 2005 (Bertrand *et al.*, 2005). The Public Health Agency of Canada's National Advisory Committee on fetal alcohol spectrum disorder issued a set of diagnostic guidelines (Chudley *et al.*, 2005) which combined the Institute of Medicine criteria and the four-digit diagnostic code. They emphasised a full exploration of all possible causes ('a diagnosis of exclusion'), and recommended neurobehavioural assessment across nine independent domains: sensory–motor signs, brain structure, cognition, communication, academic achievement, memory, executive functioning, attention, and adaptive behaviour (Benz *et al.*, 2009). Benz and colleagues (2009) considered these guidelines an improvement on the Institute of Medicine guidelines and the four-digit code. However, the four-digit diagnostic code (Astley, 2004) is still widely used. This tool allows assessment across four categories of FASD-related impairment – growth deficiency, FAS facial features, CNS damage or dysfunction, and prenatal alcohol exposure – resulting in nine distinct diagnostic outcomes across the fetal alcohol spectrum.

Identification of fetal alcohol spectrum disorder

The majority of CYP affected by prenatal alcohol exposure do not meet the physical criteria for an FAS diagnosis (Astley *et al.*, 2002). However, with evidence of the mother's alcohol intake during pregnancy and detailed historical, biological, social, and physiological evidence, it is possible to identify CYP on the wider fetal alcohol spectrum without the presence of facial features (Mukherjee *et al.*, 2005; Gray and Mukherjee, 2007). In addition to FAS, the US Institute of Medicine recognises 'alcohol-related effects', more commonly known as 'fetal alcohol effects' – these are other conditions related to proven fetal alcohol exposure which have some CNS dysfunctions but may not have the associated facial and/or growth differences (Rasmussen, 2005):

- *Alcohol-related birth defects (ARBDs)* – Those affected will not have facial differences or delayed growth and development, but will have physical anomalies such as organ (e.g.

heart, kidney) malformations, skeletal problems, and/or sensory impairments (Hoyme *et al.*, 2005; Gahagan *et al.*, 2006).

- *Alcohol-related neurodevelopmental disorder (ARND)* – Those affected will have normal growth and structural development, but will display neurobehavioural or cognitive abnormalities characteristic of prenatal alcohol exposure which cannot be explained by inherited traits or environmental influences (Hoyme *et al.*, 2005). CYP with ARND show markedly impaired executive functioning on complex tasks in all areas, but can perform in the normal range on simple tests (Hoyme *et al.*, 2005).

Among the children of heavy-drinking mothers, those with FAEs outnumber those with FAS by three to one (Mattson and Riley, 2011).

It is thought that many CYP with FAEs go unrecognised (see the section on 'Underdiagnosis' below) although their CNS difficulties can be as severe as or worse than those of CYP with FAS (Rasmussen, 2005). The high level of adoption and fostering of CYP with FASDs means that the birth mother's alcohol use during pregnancy is often unknown. Where it is known, the birth family's feelings of guilt and stigma may lead to inaccurate recall by birth families of maternal drinking levels during pregnancy. Therefore, as identification can be made only with knowledge of the mother's drinking during pregnancy, often FASDs can be only suspected and not confirmed.

As a result of these difficulties, attempts are being made to identify a distinct set of neuropsychological or behavioural characteristics which will enable FASDs to be diagnosed without the need to confirm the mother's alcohol intake during pregnancy (Mattson and Riley, 2011; Warren *et al.*, 2011). Gray and colleagues (2009) suggest that there might be more than one such profile associated with FASDs. However, the similarities between difficulties associated with FAS/FASDs and other conditions, and the variations within the FASD population within categories (Astley, 2009), have made some researchers doubt whether it will be possible to discover a distinctive profile associated with the wider spectrum conditions. Gibbard (2009, p. 27), in a recent exploration of FASD literature, found that functional deficits associated with FASDs spanned 'every possible neuropsychological domain'.

However, even if not distinctive, Mattson and Riley (2011) argue that neurodevelopmental profiles may be useful in improved understanding of the disorder, and indicating appropriate evidence-based interventions, based on areas of relative strength, which target areas of relative weakness. They go on to suggest:

> For example, if remediation targeted memory impairment, it would be beneficial to understand that children with FASD have greater problems with learning than with recall of learned information and therefore may benefit from repeated exposure to new information.
>
> (Mattson and Riley, 2011, p. 52)

Differences across the lifespan

The cognitive and behavioural profile of CYP with FASDs changes over time, so the learning needs of primary and secondary students with FASDs are subtly different. Riley (2011) notes that newborn babies with FASDs are frequently hyperreactive to stimulation and have arousal dysregulation issues. He also mentions 'high activity levels, disturbed sleep patterns, trouble feeding, and, in extreme cases, a neonatal withdrawal syndrome'. Older babies may have motor problems, developmental delay, and language and cognition issues (Riley, 2011). Learning, behavioural/emotional, and social difficulties typically become more evident as the child progresses through school. Benton Gibbard and colleagues (2003, p. 74) suggest that 'repeated neuropsychological assessment may be needed at different times during the life of an individual with FASD to capture accurately their evolving strengths and weaknesses, and to plan appropriate interventions'. Transition between primary and secondary schools needs to be carefully managed, as this is an area in which support strategies and services can often become disrupted, and communication can break down between practitioners (Ward *et al.*, 2003). For teenagers, issues around emotions, friendships and sexual behaviour, independence, and achievement compound their primary impairments (Connor and Huggins, 2005).

Advances in fetal alcohol spectrum disorder research

There continue to be positive breakthroughs in the field of FASDs. These include:

- establishing the facial characteristics from a three-dimensional computer recognition instead of using a two-dimensional photo or other methods (Warren *et al.*, 2011; Wetherill and Faroud, 2011) – this may improve diagnosis where there is no access to a trained specialist;
- identifying neurobehavioural differences in initiating eye movements during test tasks (Green *et al.*, 2007, 2009) – CYP with FASDs were found to have significantly slower eye movement initiation times than a cohort without FASDs;
- finding that measures of executive function and spatial processing are especially sensitive to prenatal alcohol exposure, which could help towards establishing a neurocognitive or neurobehavioural profile (Mattson and Riley, 2011);
- the possible effectiveness of pharmacological agents and dietary supplements to counteract prenatal alcohol-induced deficits (Kodituwakku and Kodituwakku, 2011);
- advances in understanding the mechanisms of alcohol teratogenesis (Kodituwakku and Kodituwakku, 2011);
- other areas of interest such as information processing and integration style, mathematics, and aspects of attention (Gibbard, 2009; Jonsson *et al.*, 2009).

Researchers are also working to identify earlier indications of later difficulties experienced by CYP with FASDs, in the hope that therapies can lead to more positive outcomes (Kable and Coles, 2004). Difficulties associated with FASDs in eyeblink conditioning – used to study learning and memory – and in the development of numerosity can both be identified in infancy.

Prevalence of fetal alcohol spectrum disorders

Fetal alcohol spectrum disorders can range from very mild to very severe (Gahagan *et al.*, 2006). Although there has been a lot of research on prevalence – the number or proportion of cases with a condition in a specific population – around FAS and FASDs, the accuracy of the figures is compromised by inadequate recording and identification of FASDs. This has been for a variety of reasons including (Gahagan *et al.*, 2006; Benz *et al.*, 2009; Morleo *et al.*, 2011):

- hospital recording methods;
- lack of awareness of the condition;
- poor recognition of symptoms;
- reluctance to address alcohol issues with the birth mother;
- reluctance to diagnose because of stigma and lack of targeted interventions.

In the UK, there are currently no reliable prevalence figures for FAS or FASDs as they are not routinely collected or recorded by the British Paediatric Surveillance Unit (BMA, 2007). The most quoted prevalence figure is that given by the Institute of Medicine in the USA: about 0.5–3 CYP with FAS per 1,000 of population, and, for CYP with FASDs, 10 in 1,000. However, the prevalence of FAS/FASDs is still debated, and Gray and colleagues (2009) point out the need for caution and further research before these figures can be confirmed. However, based on his current research among representative populations in Italy, May (2009) believes accepted rates for the USA and Europe are low. He states:

> We believe that the prevalence of FAS is closer to 2 to 7 per 1,000; and rather than FASD existing at 1%, we believe that the rates of FASD . . . are between 2% and 5% in the general population of developed countries.
>
> (May, 2009, p. 21)

International studies have been summarised (e.g. Gray *et al.*, 2009; Blackburn, 2010; Carpenter, 2011). Whereas rates in Australia are 0.06 per 1,000 live births, in certain very high-risk South African communities, where historically workers' wages were part-paid in alcohol, the prevalence has been estimated at 68.0–89.2 per 1,000. Golden (2005) reports 1 in 170 live births among aboriginal populations in New Zealand, Australia, and the United States. There are also high rates of FAS among populations where both men and women drink moderately but daily with meals. May and colleagues (2006) found the rates of full-blown FAS in some Italian communities were 3.7–7.4 per 1,000 CYP, and for FASDs, 20.3–40.5 per 1,000.

Among children who are fostered and adopted – a selective population – there have also been traditionally high prevalences of FAS. Astley and colleagues (2002) found that among CYP in foster care 1 to 1.5 per 100 had FAS – a prevalence which is five to ten times greater than that in the general population.

Underdiagnosis

Current prevalence figures are believed to underestimate the prevalence of FASD (Mukherjee et al., 2006). When FAS/FASD is not identified, individuals may not gain access to appropriate medical and social services. Often professionals who could initiate diagnosis or identification do not do so. This is for various reasons including (Gahagan et al., 2006; Mukherjee et al., 2006; Gray and Mukherjee, 2007; Gray et al., 2009):

- They lack knowledge around identification of FAS/FASDs.
- Alternative diagnosis is made because symptoms resemble other conditions.
- Where the condition is recognised, nothing is done about it.
- Routine screening for FAS/FASDs is lacking in prenatal and paediatric settings.
- There are no standard intervention responses to diagnosis/identification of FAS/FASDs.
- Where difficulties are identified (e.g. behavioural or learning issues), they are often not considered in the possible context of FASDs.
- They are reluctant to screen because of time constraints, fear of litigation, fear of stigmatising the family, or a sense that such a diagnosis is futile because there are no linked services.

This situation often leads to alternative diagnoses to FASDs being made based on symptoms alone (FASCETS, 2010). These may include ADHD; ASDs; Asperger syndrome; learning disabilities; global developmental delay; post-traumatic stress disorder; reactive attachment disorder (RAD); conduct disorder; social emotional behavioural disorder (SEBD); oppositional defiant disorder (ODD); and other mental health issues such as depression, anxiety, or schizophrenia (O'Malley, 2007; Dubovsky, 2009; Coles, 2011).

Dubovsky (2009) states that, if an FASD co-occurs with these disorders, this should be recognised and the intervention adapted to reflect this. Lack of an FASD diagnosis can lead to inappropriate interventions.

Only now is brain imaging beginning to confirm patterns that separate children with FASDs from other CYP with similar neurobehavioural profiles (Andrew, 2009, in Jonsson et al., 2009). Research has found that some commonly successful medicinal and behavioural interventions for ADHD are ineffective for those with FASDs, perhaps because of different underlying neurocognitive characteristics (O'Malley, 2007; Dubovsky, 2009; Coles, 2011).

The importance of diagnosis

Preventable secondary disabilities often arise from the impact of primary disabilities on CYP's life experiences (Benz et al., 2009), and the prenatal effects of alcohol on CYP's stress systems may make them particularly vulnerable (Weinberg, 2009). Researchers have emphasised the importance of diagnosis and early intervention for CYP with FASDs – preferably before the age of six years – so an early network of professional and social support can be put in place (Benz, 2009; May, 2009; Mattson and Riley, 2011). However, most CYP with FAS are diagnosed later in primary school, so the window for early intervention is missed (Novick Brown, 2011). Streissguth and colleagues (Benz, 2009) found that diagnosis, preferably before age six, reduced the risk of poor outcomes. However, appropriate intervention at any age can produce life improvements (Grant et al., 2004).

Some people feel a diagnosis of an FASD will label the child, but as SAMHSA (2010) points out:

> inaccurate diagnosis can be harmful. Persons with an undiagnosed FASD may be mislabeled as noncompliant, uncooperative, or unmotivated. In addition, treatments are selected on the basis of the diagnosis. If the diagnosis is not correct, the treatment will not be correct. For example, medications for ADHD may not help a person whose attention deficits stem from prenatal alcohol exposure.

SAMHSA (2010) identifies the possible benefits of diagnosis as:

- decreasing CYP's frustration and anger at not being like others their age;
- decreasing the frustration and anger of caregivers toward the child;
- appropriate interventions (e.g. in school, vocational services, treatment, corrections);
- identifying families who may need future prenatal support.

Without diagnosis, a lack of awareness by professionals and families of CYP's difficulties can lead to consistently unrealistic expectations of them (Streissguth and O'Malley, 2000). This may lead to the CYP developing serious defensive behavioural, cognitive, and psychological secondary disabilities. These can include mental health problems (seen in 87% of children; O'Connor et al., 2002), disrupted school experience (60% over the age of 11 years; Riley, 2003); trouble with the law (60% of teenagers; Kelly, 2009), confinement (50%; Kelly, 2009), inappropriate sexual behaviour, and problems with dependent living (80%; Riley, 2003) and employment (Streissguth and Kanter, 1997). They are also at increased risk of developing addictive behaviours such as alcohol abuse, thereby potentially continuing the cycle of FASDs into the next generation (Baer et al., 2003). Streissguth and colleagues (1996) found that 3 per cent of 6- to 11-year-olds, 12 per cent of 12- to 20-year-olds, and 23 per cent of adults from a cohort of 415 subjects diagnosed with FAS or FAEs had attempted suicide. (The adult figure is five times the US national average.)

The educational advantage of identifying FAS/FASD for the individual is that it can trigger support for specific areas of difficulty known to be linked with FASDs. A diagnosis or identification increases the sensitisation of professionals to CYP's needs and characteristics related to their condition. As Fetal Alcohol Syndrome Consultation, Education and Training Services, Inc. (FASCETS) states on its website: 'Knowledge about FASD and organicity provides a way to shift perceptions'.

Myles Himmelreich, Director of Programming, Canadian FASD Foundation, describes what it is like to have an FASD:

> The fact is that not only can the people around a person with FASD not see or note anything special, but the individuals with FASD do not see it themselves. They do not see something that jumps out to say, 'Yes, you have a disability and that is why you have these struggles; that is why you have these issues.' . . . I looked in the mirror and did not see anything to say, 'It is okay, because you have FASD; that is why you are having these problems.' I just saw somebody that looked like a regular kid . . . It was a huge learning curve for me to understand that I need support and help and that I am going to have ups and downs and struggles because I have FASD.
>
> (Himmelreich, 2009, p. 9)

A diagnosis/identification is important for CYP. Without it, they can be constantly ambushed by their difficulties in the form of an ever-increasing list of things they cannot achieve. Diagnosis gives identity, which they can align themselves with or struggle against. It provides an overarching term for their difficulties and provides a benchmark against which they can gain a sense of success. It enables them, their family, and professionals to predict possible outcomes and circumvent difficulties. It allows parents and educators to be realistic in their expectations and properly celebratory of achievements. It gives CYP and families a community of others like them, who find life difficult in similar ways.

> [T]here is a feeling that 'I'm not the problem; I have a problem.' I think that is powerful for the affected individual, and it helps the caregivers not to blame themselves for not being good enough parents, to realize that they are dealing with a brain that has differences.
>
> (Andrew, 2009)

Conclusion

The disabilities caused by alcohol are permanent and lifelong. Physical features may become less after puberty, but intellectual impairments remain a challenge, and, without informed and understanding support, emotional, behavioural, and social problems often get worse (National Institutes of Health, 2007). CYP born with alcohol-related disabilities, and their families, have to struggle with not only the impact of those disabilities, but also the misunderstandings and unrealistic expectations of people who do not realise their impact.

Although there is no cure for FASDs, research shows that there are effective interventions (Chandrasena *et al.* 2009). Educators will undoubtedly meet CYP with FASDs in their classrooms. They need to know how to respond to their learning needs effectively, enabling them to maximise their potential, improve their life chances, and take their places alongside their unaffected peers as citizens. To do this, teaching staff will need training and support.

References

Abel, E.L. (1997) 'Was fetal alcohol syndrome recognized in the ancient Near East?', *Alcohol and Alcoholism*, 32 (1): 3–7. Online at: http://alcalc.oxfordjournals.org/content/32/1/3.full.pdf+html, accessed 17 September 2011.

Abel, E.L. (1999a) 'Was the fetal alcohol syndrome recognized by the Greeks and Romans?', *Alcohol and Alcoholism*, 34 (6): 868–872. Online at: http://alcalc.oxfordjournals.org/content/34/6/868.full.pdf+html, accessed 17 September 2011.

Abel, E.L. (1999b) '"Who goes to bed drunk begets but a girl": The history of a Renaissance medical proverb', *Journal of the History of Medicine*, 54: 5–22.

Abel, E.L. (2001) 'Gin Lane: did Hogarth know about fetal alcohol syndrome?', *Alcohol and Alcoholism*, 36 (2): 131–134. Online at: http://alcalc.oxfordjournals.org/content/36/2/131.full.pdf+html, accessed 17 September 2011.

Andrew, G. (2009) 'Overview of FASD', in Jonsson, E., Dennett, L., and Littlejohn, G. (eds) *Fetal Alcohol Spectrum Disorder (FASD): Across the Lifespan (Proceedings from an IHE Consensus Development Conference 2009)*. Edmonton, Canada: Institute of Health Economics. Online at: www.ihe.ca/documents/FASDproceedings.pdf, accessed 17 September 2011.

Astley, S.J. (2004) *Diagnostic Guide for Fetal Alcohol Spectrum Disorders: The 4-Digit Diagnostic Code (3rd edn)*. Washington, DC: Center on Human Development and Disability, University of Washington. Online at: http://depts.washington.edu/fasdpn/htmls/4-digit-code.htm, accessed 25 September 2011.

Astley, S.J. (2009) 'Prevalence of FAS in foster care', in Jonsson, E., Dennett, L., and Littlejohn, G. (eds) *Fetal Alcohol Spectrum Disorder (FASD): Across the Lifespan (Proceedings from an IHE Consensus Development Conference 2009)*. Edmonton, Canada: Institute of Health Economics. Online at: www.ihe.ca/documents/FASDproceedings.pdf, accessed 17 September 2011.

Astley, S.J. and Clarren, S.K. (2000) 'Diagnosing the full spectrum of fetal alcohol-exposed individuals: introducing the 4-digit diagnostic code', *Alcohol and Alcoholism,* 35 (4), 400–410. Online at: http://alcalc.oxfordjournals.org/content/35/4/400.full.pdf+html, accessed 16 September 2011.

Astley, S.J., Bailey, D., Talbot, C., and Clarren, S.K. (2000a) 'Fetal alcohol syndrome (FAS) primary prevention through FAS diagnosis: I. Identification of high-risk birth mothers through the diagnosis of their children', *Alcohol and Alcoholism*, 35 (5): 499–508. Online at: www.ncbi.nlm.nih.gov/pubmed/11022025, accessed 17 September 2011.

Astley, S.J., Bailey, D., Talbot, C. and Clarren, S.K. (2000b) 'Fetal alcohol syndrome (FAS) primary prevention through FAS diagnosis: II. A comprehensive profile of 80 birth mothers of children with FAS', *Alcohol and Alcoholism*, 35 (5): 509–519. Online at: http://alcalc.oxfordjournals.org/content/35/5/509.full, accessed 17 September 2011.

Astley, S.J., Stachowiak, J., Clarren, S.K., and Clausen, C. (2002) 'Application of the fetal alcohol syndrome facial photographic screening tool in a foster care population', *Journal of Pediatrics*, 141 (5): 712–717. Online at: http://depts.washington.edu/fasdpn/pdfs/foster.pdf, accessed 10 September 2011.

Baer, J.S., Sampson, P.D., Barr, H.M., Connor, P.D., and Streissguth, A.P. (2003) 'A 21 year longitudinal analysis of the effects of prenatal exposure on young adult drinking', *Archives of General Psychiatry*, 60 (April): 377–385.

BBC One (Cambridgeshire, East) (2009) 'Julie Reinger meets the families living with the consequences of Foetal Alcohol Syndrome', *Inside Out,* 23 November, 19:30.

Benz, J., Rasmussen, C., and Andrew, K. (2009) 'Diagnosing fetal alcohol spectrum disorder: history, challenges and future directions', *Paediatric Child Health*, 14 (4): 231–237.

Benton Gibbard, W., Wass, P., and Clarke, M.E. (2003) 'The neuropsychological implications of prenatal alcohol exposure', *Canadian Child and Adolescent Psychiatry Review*, 12 (3): 72–76.

Bertrand, J., Floyd, R.L., and Weber, M.K. (2005) 'Guidelines for identifying and referring persons with fetal alcohol syndrome', *Morbity and Mortality Weekly Report*, 54 (RR-11): 1–10. Online at: www.cdc.gov/mmwr/pdf/rr/rr5411.pdf, accessed 25 September 2011.

Blackburn, C. (2010) *Facing the Challenge and Shaping the Future for Primary and Secondary Aged Students with Foetal Alcohol Spectrum Disorders* (FAS-eD Project). London: NOFAS-UK. Online at: http://www.nofas-uk.org/news.htm#tdanews, accessed 16 September 2011.

British Liver Trust (2010) *Alcohol and Liver Disease.* Ringwood: British Liver Trust. Online at: www.britishlivertrust.org.uk/home/the-liver/liver-diseases/alcohol.aspx, accessed 27 September 2011.

BMA (British Medical Association) (2007) *Fetal Alcohol Spectrum Disorders: A Guide for Healthcare Professionals.* London: British Medical Association.

Carpenter, B. (2011) 'Pedagogically bereft: improving learning outcomes for children with Foetal Alcohol Spectrum Disorders', *British Journal of Special Education*, 38 (1): 37–43.

Chandrasena, A.N., Mukherjee, R.A.S., and Turk, J. (2009) 'Fetal alcohol spectrum disorders: an overview of interventions for affected individuals', *Child and Adolescent Mental Health*, 14: 162–167.

Christiaens, L., Mizon J.P., and Delmarie, G. (1960) 'Sur la descendance des alcooliques', *Annales de Pediatrie*, 36: 37–42.

Chudley, A.E., Conry, J., Cook, J.L., Loock, C., Rosales, T., and LeBlanc, N. (2005) 'Fetal alcohol spectrum disorders: Canadian guidelines for diagnosis', *Canadian Medical Association Journal*, 172 (5 suppl.): S1–S21. Online at: www.cmaj.ca/content/172/5_suppl/S1.full.pdf, accessed 17 September 2011.

Coles, C.D. (2011) 'Discriminating the effects of prenatal alcohol exposure from other behavioral and learning disorders', *Alcohol Research and Health*, 34 (1): 42–50. Online at: http://pubs.niaaa.nih.gov/publications/arh341/42-50.htm, accessed 26 September 2011.

Connor, P.D. and Huggins, J. (2005) 'Prenatal development: fetal alcohol spectrum disorders', in Thies, K. (ed.) *Handbook of Human Development for Healthcare Professionals.* Sudbury, MA: Jones and Bartlett. Online at: http://books.google.co.uk/books?id=CkbMiPxwvBQC, accessed 20 April 2009.

Department of Health (2009) 'FOI: alcohol and pregnancy message'. Online at: http://www.dh.gov.uk/en/FreedomOfInformation/Freedomofinformationpublicationschemefeedback/FOIreleases/DH_100220, accessed 26 February 2012.

Dubovsky, D. (2009) 'Co-morbidities with mental health for an individual with FASD', in Jonsson, E., Dennett, L., and Littlejohn, G. (eds) *Fetal Alcohol Spectrum Disorder (FASD): Across the Lifespan (Proceedings from an IHE Consensus Development Conference 2009)*. Edmonton, Canada: Institute of Health Economics. Online at: www.ihe.ca/documents/FASDproceedings.pdf, accessed 17 September 2011.

FASCETS (Fetal Alcohol Syndrome Consultation, Education and Training Services, Inc.) (2010) 'FASCETS conceptual foundation: a neurobehavioral construct for interventions for children and adults with fetal alcohol spectrum disorders (FASD)'; 'Understanding FASD (Fetal Alcohol Spectrum Disorders)'. Online at: http://www.fascets.org/, accessed 11 September 2011.

Gahagan, S., Telfair Sharpe, T., Brimacombe, M., Fry-Johnson, Y., Levine, R., Mengel, M., O'Connor, M., Paley, B., Adubatu, S., and Brenneman, G. (2006) 'Paediatricians' knowledge, training, and experience in the care of children with fetal alcohol spectrum', *Journal of Pediatrics*, 118 (3): e657–e668. Online at: http://pediatrics.aappublications.org/content/118/3/e657.full.pdf, accessed 10 September 2011.

Gibbard, B. (2009) 'Extent and impact on child development', in Jonsson, E., Dennett, L., and Littlejohn, G. (eds) *Fetal Alcohol Spectrum Disorder (FASD): Across the Lifespan (Proceedings from an IHE Consensus Development Conference 2009)*. Edmonton, Canada: Institute of Health Economics. Online at: http://www.ihe.ca/documents/FASDproceedings.pdf, accessed 17 September 2011.

Golden, J.L. (2005) *Message in a Bottle: The Making of Fetal Alcohol Syndrome*. Cambridge, MA: Harvard University Press.

Grant, T., Huggins, J., Connor, P., Pedersen, J.Y., Whitney, N., and Streissguth, A. (2004) 'A pilot community intervention for young women with fetal alcohol spectrum disorders', *Journal of Community Mental Health*, 40: 499–511.

Gray, R. and Mukherjee, R.A.S. (2007) 'A psychiatrist's guide to fetal alcohol spectrum disorders in mothers who drunk heavily during pregnancy', *Advances in Mental Health and Learning Disabilities*, 1: 19–26.

Gray, R., Mukherjee, R.A.S., and Rutter, M. (2009) 'Alcohol consumption during pregnancy and its effects on neurodevelopment: what is known and what remains uncertain', *Addiction*, 104: 1270–1273.

Green, C.R., Munoz, D.P., Nikkel, S.M., and Reynolds, J.N. (2007) 'Deficits in eye movement control in children with fetal alcohol spectrum disorders', *Alcoholism: Clinical and Experimental Research*, 31 (3): 500–511.

Green, C.R., Mihic, A.M., Brien, D.C., Armstrong, I.T., Nikkel, S.M., Stade, B.C., Rasmussen, C., Munoz, D.P., and Reynolds, J.N. (2009) 'Oculomotor control in children with fetal alcohol spectrum disorders assessed using a mobile eye-tracking laboratory', *European Journal of Neuroscience*, 29 (6): 1302–1309.

Heuyer, H., Mises, R., and Dereux, J.F. (1957) 'La descendance des alcooliques', *Nouvelle Presse Medicale*, 29: 657–658.

Himmelreich, M. (2009) 'A personal perspective', in Jonsson, E., Dennett, L., and Littlejohn, G. (eds) *Fetal Alcohol Spectrum Disorder (FASD): Across the Lifespan (Proceedings from an IHE Consensus Development Conference 2009)*. Edmonton, Canada: Institute of Health Economics. Online at: www.ihe.ca/documents/FASDproceedings.pdf, accessed 17 September 2011.

Hoyme, H.E., May, P.A., Kalberg, W.O., Kodituwakku, P., Gossage, J.P., Trujillo, P.M., Buckley, D.G., Miller, J.H., Aragon, A.S., Khaole, N., Viljoen, D.L., Jones, K.L., and Robinson. L.K. (2005) 'Clarification of the 1996 Institute of Medicine criteria: a practical clinical approach to diagnosis of fetal alcohol spectrum disorders', *Pediatrics*, 115 (1): 39–47.

Jacobson, S.W., Jacobson, J.L., Sokol, R.J., Chiodo, L.M., and Corobana, R. (2004) 'Maternal age, alcohol abuse history, and quality of parenting as moderators of the effects of prenatal alcohol exposure on 7.5-year intellectual function', *Alcohol: Clinical and Experimental Research*, 28: 1732–1745.

Jones, K.L. and Smith, D.W. (1973) 'Recognition of the fetal alcohol syndrome in early infancy', *Lancet*, 2 (7836): 999–1001.

Jonsson, E., Dennett, L., and Littlejohn, G. (eds) (2009) *Fetal Alcohol Spectrum Disorder (FASD): Across the Lifespan (Proceedings from an IHE Consensus Development Conference 2009)*. Edmonton, Canada: Institute of Health Economics. Online at: www.ihe.ca/documents/FASDproceedings.pdf, accessed 17 September 2011.

Kable, J.A. and Coles, C.D. (2004) 'The impact of prenatal alcohol exposure on neurophysiological encoding of environmental events at six months', *Alcohol: Clinical and Experimental Research*, 28: 489–496.

Kelly, K. (2009) 'Is Foetal Alcohol Spectrum Disorder linked to anti-social behaviour?', *Woman's Hour*, Radio 4. Online at: www.bbc.co.uk/radio4/womanshour/03/2009_16_mon.shtml, accessed 20 April 2009.

Kelly, Y., Sacker, A., Gray, R., Kelly, J., Wolke, D., and Quigley, M.A. (2009) 'Light drinking in pregnancy, a risk for behavioural problems and cognitive deficits at 3 years of age?', *International Journal of Epidemiology*, 38: 129–140.

Kodituwakku, P.W. and Kodituwakku, F.I. (2011) 'From research to practice: an integrative framework for the development of interventions for children with fetal alcohol spectrum disorders', *Neuropsychology Review*, 21 (2): 204–223. Online at: http://fetalalcoholsyndrome.researchtoday.net/, accessed 22 September 2011.

Kulaga, V. (2009) 'Fatty Acid Ethyl Esters (FAEE), a biomarker of alcohol exposure: hope for a silent epidemic of fetal alcohol affected children' (PhD thesis). Toronto, Canada: University of Toronto. Online at: https://tspace.library.utoronto.ca/bitstream/1807/17788/1/Kulaga_Vivian_A_200906_PhD_thesis.pdf, accessed 17 September 2011.

Lebel, C., Roussotte, F., and Sowell, E.R. (2011) 'Imaging the impact of prenatal alcohol exposure on the structure of the developing human brain', *Neuropsychology Review*, 21: 102–118. Online at: http://fetalalcoholsyndrome.researchtoday.net/, accessed 22 September 2011.

Lemoine, P., Harouusseau, H., Borteyru, J.P., and Menuet, J.-C. (1968) 'Les enfants de parents alcooliques: anomalies observées, à propos de 127 cas', Ouest Médical, 21: 476–482.

Luu, T.N. (2010) 'A rat model of fetal alcohol syndrome: molecular and behavioural analysis' (Masters thesis). New Brunswick, NJ: Rutgers University. Online at: http://www.grin.com/en/doc/248543/a-rat-model-of-fetal-alcohol-syndrome-molecular-and-behavioral-analysis, accessed 10 September 2011.

Maier, S.E. and West, J.R. (2001) 'Drinking patterns and alcohol-related birth defects', *Alcohol Research and Health*, 25 (3): 168–174.

March of Dimes (2008) 'Drinking alcohol during pregnancy'. Online at: www.marchofdimes.com/alcohol_indepth.html, accessed 25 September 2011.

Mattson, S.N. and Riley, E.P. (2011) 'The quest for a neurodevelopmental profile of heavy prenatal alcohol exposure', *Alcohol Research and Health*, 34 (1): 51–55.

May, P. (2009) 'Prevalence and incidence internationally', in Jonsson, E., Dennett, L., and Littlejohn, G. (eds) *Fetal Alcohol Spectrum Disorder (FASD): Across the Lifespan (Proceedings from an IHE Consensus Development Conference 2009)*. Edmonton, Canada: Institute of Health Economics. Online at: http://www.ihe.ca/documents/FASDproceedings.pdf, accessed 17 September 2011.

May, P.A., Fiorentino, D., Coriale, G., Kalberg, W.O., Hoyme, E.H., Aragón, A.S., Buckley, D., Stellavato, C., Gossage, J.P., Robinson, L.K., Lyons Jones, K., Manning, M., and Ceccanti, M. (2011) 'Prevalence of children with severe fetal alcohol spectrum disorders in communities near Rome, Italy: new estimated rates are higher than previous estimates', *International Journal of Environmental Research and Public Health*, 8 (6): 2331–2351. Online at: http://www.ncbi.nlm.nih.gov/pmc/articles/PMC3138028/pdf/ijerph-08-02331.pdf, accessed 25 September 2011.

Moore, K.L. and Persaud, T.V.N. (1993) *The Developing Human: Clinically Oriented Embryology*. Philadelphia: W.B. Saunders.

Morleo, M., Woolfall, K., Dedman, D., Mukherjee, R., Bellis, M.A., and Cook, P. (2011) 'Under-reporting of foetal alcohol spectrum disorders: an analysis of hospital episode statistics', *BMC Pediatrics*, 11 (14).

Mukherjee, R.A.S., Hollins, S., and Abou-Saleh, M.T. (2005) 'Low level alcohol consumption and the fetus', *British Medical Journal*, 330: 375–376.

Mukherjee, R.A.S., Hollins, S., and Turk, J. (2006) 'Fetal alcohol spectrum disorder: an overview', *Journal of the Royal Society of Medicine*, 99: 298–302. Online at: www.intellectualdisability.info/mental_phys_health/fetal_alcohol_mukherjee.htm, accessed 19 April 2009.

National Institutes of Health (2007) 'Information about alcohol' (NIH Curriculum Supplement Series). Bethesda, MD: National Institutes of Health. Online at: http://www.ncbi.nlm.nih.gov/books/NBK20630, accessed 12 January 2012.

National Organization on Fetal Alchohol Syndrome (2004) *Fetal Development Chart*. Online at: www.nofas.org/healthcare/QIP%20Materials/Patient%20Education%20Materials/Fetal%20Development%20Chart%20Outline.pdf, accessed 2 April 2012.

NOFAS-UK (2010) 'Fetal Alcohol Spectrum Disorder: CPD accredited online course'. Online at: www.nofas-uk.org/OnlineCourse/USING/using_the_course_frame.php.htm, accessed 11 September 2011.

Novik Brown, N. (2011) 'Evidence-based interventions with children Fetal Alcohol Spectrum Disorders', *Paradigm*, Spring: 12–17. Online at: www.nofas-uk.org/PDF/Fetal%20Alcohol%20Forum%20Issue%205.pdf (within Fetal Alcohol Forum), accessed 11 September 2011.

O'Connor, M.J., Shah, B., Whaley, S., Cronin, P., Gunderson, B., and Graham, J. (2002) 'Psychiatric illness in a clinical sample of children with prenatal alcohol exposure', *American Journal of Drug and Alcohol Abuse*, 28: 743–754.

O'Connor, M.J., Frankel, F., Paley, P., Schonfeld, A.M., Carpenter, E., Laugeson, E.A., and Marquardt, R. (2006) 'A controlled social skills training for children with Fetal Alcohol Spectrum Disorders', *Journal of Consulting and Clinical Psychology*, 74 (4): 639–648.

O'Malley, K. (2007) *ADHD and Fetal Alcohol Spectrum Disorders*. Hauppauge, NY: Nova Science Publishers.

Plant, M.L. (1985) *Women, Drinking and Pregnancy*. London: Tavistock.

Public Health Agency of Canada (2010) *Early Primary School Outcomes Associated with Maternal Use of Alcohol and Tobacco during Pregnancy and with Exposure to Parent Alcohol and Tobacco Use Postnatally*. Ottawa, Canada: Public Health Agency of Canada.

Rasmussen, C. (2005) 'Executive functioning and working memory in fetal alcohol spectrum disorder', *Alcoholism: Clinical and Experimental Research*, 29 (8): 1359–1367.

Riley, E. (2003) 'FAE/FAS: prevention, intervention and support services: commentary on Burd and Juelson, Coles and O'Malley and Stressguth', in Tremblay, R.E., Barr, R.G., and Peters, R.D.V (eds) *Online Encyclopaedia on Early Childhood Development*. Online at: www.child-encyclopedia.com/documents/RileyANGxp.pdf, accessed 14 June 2010.

Riley, E. (2011) 'Foetal alcohol syndrome', *Web Chats* (6 July). Hosted by the National Organization on Fetal Alcohol Syndrome (NOFAS). Online at: http://www.talkingalcohol.com/index.asp?pageid=134, accessed 9 September 2011.

Riley, E.P., Infante, M.A., and Warren, K.R. (2011) 'Fetal alcohol spectrum disorders: an overview', *Neuropsychology Review*, 21 (2): 73–80.

Rouquette, J. (1957) 'Influence of paternal alcoholic toxicomania on the psychic development of young children' (unpublished medical thesis). Paris, France: University of Paris.

Spedding, J., Ellis, R.L., and Heath, D.D. (eds) (1857–1859) *The Works of Francis Bacon, Vol. 5*. Boston: Houghton Mifflin. Online at: http://www.archive.org/stream/worksfrancisbaco05bacoiala/worksfrancisbaco05bacoiala_djvu.txt, accessed 15 September 2011.

Streissguth, A. and Kanter, J. (eds) (1997) *The Challenges of Fetal Alcohol Syndrome: Overcoming Secondary Disabilities*. Seattle: University of Washington Press.

Streissguth, A.P. and O'Malley, K. (2000) 'Neuropsychiatric implications and long-term consequences of fetal alcohol spectrum disorders', *Seminars in Clinical Neuropsychiatry*, 5 (3): 177–190.

Streissguth, A., Barr, H., Kogan, J., and Bookstein, F. (1996) *Understanding the Occurrence of Secondary Disabilities in Clients with Fetal Alcohol Syndrome (FAS) and Fetal Alcohol Effects* (FAE Final Report: Centers for Disease Control and Prevention Grant No. 04/CCR008515). Seattle, WA: University of Washington Fetal Alcohol and Drug Unit.

SAMHSA (Substance Abuse and Mental Health Services Administration) (2010) 'Fetal Alcohol Spectrum Disorders (FASD): The basics' (PowerPoint presentation). Online at: www.fasdcenter.samhsa.gov/educationTraining/fasdBasics.cfm, accessed 11 September 2011.

University of Chicago (2009) 'Greek texts and translations: Plato's *Laws*'. Online at: http://perseus.uchicago.edu/perseus-cgi/citequery3.pl?dbname=GreekFeb2011&getid=1&query=Pl.%20Leg.%20776a, accessed 15 September 2011.

US Department of Health and Human Services, Centers for Disease Control and Prevention, National Center on Birth Defects and Developmental Disabilities, FASD Regional Training Centers, and the National Organisation of Fetal Alcohol Syndrome (2008) *Fetal Alcohol Spectrum Disorders Competency-Based Curriculum Development Guide for Medical and Allied Health Education and Practice*. Online at: http://www.cdc.gov/ncbddd/fasd/curriculum/FASDguide_web.pdf, accessed 22 September 2011.

Vaux, K.K. (2010) 'Fetal alcohol syndrome'. Online at: http://emedicine.medscape.com/article/974016-overview, accessed 19 September 2011.

Ward, L., Mallett, R., Heslop, P., and Simons, K. (2003) 'Transition planning: how well does it work for young people with learning disabilities and their families?', *British Journal of Special Education*, 30 (3): 132–137.

Warren, K.R., Hewitt, B.G., and Thomas, J.D. (2011) 'Fetal alcohol spectrum disorders: research challenges and opportunities', *Alcohol Research and Health*, 34 (1): 4–14.

Weinberg, J. (2009) 'Direct and indirect mechanisms for alcohol damage to the brain', in Jonsson, E., Dennett, L., and Littlejohn, G. (eds) *Fetal Alcohol Spectrum Disorder (FASD): Across the Lifespan (Proceedings from an IHE Consensus Development Conference 2009)*. Edmonton, Canada: Institute of Health Economics. Online at: www.ihe.ca/documents/FASDproceedings.pdf, accessed 17 September 2011.

West, J.R. and Blake, A.C. (2005) 'Fetal alcohol syndrome: an assessment of the field', *Experimental Biology and Medicine*, 230: 354–356. Online at: http://ebm.rsmjournals.com/content/230/6/354.full.pdf, accessed 25 September 2011.

Wetherill, L. and Faroud, T. (2011) 'Understanding the effects of prenatal alcohol exposure using three-dimensional facial imaging', *Alcohol Research and Health*, 34 (1): 38–41. Online at: http://pubs.niaaa.nih.gov/publications/arh341/38-41.pdf, accessed 26 September 2011.

World Health Organization (2011) *International Classification of Diseases: 10th revision, clinical modification (ICD-10-CM)*. Geneva: WHO. Online at: www.icd10data.com/ICD10CM/Codes/Q00-Q99/Q80-Q89/Q86-/Q86.0, accessed 20 September 2011.

Chapter 3

Understanding how fetal alcohol spectrum disorders impact on learning

Children and young people (CYP) with fetal alcohol spectrum disorders (FASDs) experience a range of developmental, learning, behavioural, social, emotional, and sensory difficulties which create barriers to learning. These have an impact not only within the educational context, but also on the subsequent acquisition of crucial life skills (such as telling the time or self organisation). However, it is important to set the learning difficulties of CYP with FASDs in the context of their strengths.

Children and young people with FASDs have stated ambitions (see Blackburn, 2010) and have a range of practical strengths which are useful in their educational careers and throughout life. Many are articulate and have engaging personalities. They enjoy being with other people. Although they have working/short-term memory difficulties, rote learning and long-term memory can be strengths. Many children with FASDs have learning strengths around literacy and practical subjects, such as art, performing arts, sport, and technologies, although they often have difficulties with comprehension. These strengths will become the foundations on which to develop personalised curricula, to encourage and develop further strengths, and to build emotional resilience.

An understanding of the difficulties experienced by CYP with FASDs will help educators to recognise the steps they may need to take in order to enhance learning opportunities. Table 3.1 outlines how damage caused by alcohol to a baby's developing brain in the womb impacts on learning throughout life.

This damage results in difficulties for CYP with FASDs in many areas of the curriculum, in the acquisition of new information, linking new information to previously learned information, and the practical application of knowledge gained. Specifically, CYP with FASDs may experience difficulties in the following areas.

Developmental difficulties

- Significant delays in achieving developmental milestones such as toileting and hygiene skills, in some cases beyond the primary years.

Table 3.1 An overview of the cognitive effects of damage to different regions of the brain commonly compromised by FASDs

Area of brain damaged	Area of learning affected
Amygdala	Ability to regulate reactions with the environment such as whether to attack or escape Decision making
Basal ganglia	Initiation and modulation of motor activity Motor timing behaviours, specifically difficulty in producing accurate and consistent motor responses when intercepting a moving target or moving through a spatial target in a specified amount of time Cognitive functioning
Caudate nucleus	Regulation of the transmission of information regarding worrying events or ideas between the thalamus and the orbitofrontal cortex Effects on learning and memory as well as threshold control activities
Cerebellum	Postural control, gait, balance, and the co-ordination of bilateral movements Behaviour and memory
Corpus callosum	Speed of processing Connecting two sides of the brain
Frontal lobe	Executive function Co-ordination Processing and labelling/memory Focusing and shifting attention Planning Understanding consequences
Globus pallidus, accumbens, thalamus, cortex circuit	Decision making
Hippocampus	Ability to consolidate new memories General learning and emotional regulation
Nucleus accumbens	Links to reward, pleasure, laughter, addiction, aggression, fear, and the placebo effect
Parietal lobe	Spatial awareness Mathematical ability Dyspraxia

Source: Kellerman, 2008; Blaschke *et al.*, 2009; R. Mukherjee, personal communication, 2009 in Blackburn *et al.*, 2009.

Medical difficulties

• Medical and health-related difficulties including organ damage, poor sleep patterns, eating and dietary difficulties, small stature, vision and hearing impairments.

I've always wanted somebody to come along and say, 'I'm going to look at this child with FAS as a child with severe medical problems.' We've had so many medical professionals involved . . . not many of them have known enough about FASD to say this is standard procedure with a child with this problem.

(Parent interview, Blackburn, 2010, p. 33)

Learning difficulties

- Understanding cause and effect.
- Speech, language, and communication delays/disorders including verbosity, poor understanding, poor social cognition and communication skills, and difficulty using sophisticated language in social contexts.
- Cognitive difficulties, including poor short-term memory and poor concentration.
- Difficulty in understanding mathematical concepts, such as time, or understanding money.
- Frontal lobe damage to the brain, which is associated with FASDs, results in impaired executive functioning leading to deficits, such as impaired ability to organise, plan, understand consequences, maintain and shift attention, and process and memorise data. This has an impact on independence in a range of situations. Executive functioning impacts on daily living skills.

Behavioural difficulties

- Behavioural difficulties, including hyperactivity, inattention, aggression, obsessions with people and objects, and agitation, can cause anxiety and frustration for CYP as well as parents and educators. These difficulties, although often seen as behavioural issues, can also be related to sensory processing disorders (SPDs), requiring occupational therapy input:

In science we're hitting difficulties because of her impulsivity around behaviour, she's very drawn to the apparatus, she likes anything that's very pretty and sparkly and if you've got colourful flames and splints and nice things bubbling in jars that's a temptation for her, she wants to get in there with her hands.

(Teacher in a secondary school, Blackburn, 2010, p. 9)

Social difficulties

- Difficulty acquiring appropriate social and emotional skills, which impacts on relationships, friendships, and any activity that requires an understanding of the state of mind of others and predicting how this might affect their actions.
- Understanding boundaries: CYP can be frustrated by their own behaviour, but seemingly unable to control it, leading to challenges in self esteem and peer relationships.

She's not always aware of the impact of her behaviours on others and that upsets her, because after the event when people explain to her, she's very apologetic. She doesn't like to be like that but at the same time, she really cannot control it. This is the paradox, she's aware that she can't control herself and that's frustrating for her.

(Teacher in a secondary school, Blackburn, 2010, p. 10)

Emotional difficulties

- The need to rely on external prompts from adults can result in low self esteem and frustration.
- CYP begin to identify the differences between themselves and peers (and vice versa) even in special school settings, again resulting in low self esteem.
- Secondary disabilities, such as mental health problems, disrupted school experience, trouble with the law, confinement, inappropriate sexual behaviour, and problems with independent living and employment can result from a lack of identification/support when children are at primary age.

> I'm not sure if you could call them friends, I have people I hang around with if you know what I mean, but they're not like friends, I'm always falling out with them.
>
> (Girl aged 13, Blackburn, 2010, p. 39)

> It's almost as if he peaked in year 4 and hasn't developed much since then. The others in his class are now just as verbal as him but their understanding of things is much higher. The other students are now almost anti-Collin[1] now because he's so immature compared to them and what they're expecting of their peers he's not reaching, so they have shunned him, we have to have sessions to deal with this as they are now bullying him.
>
> (Teacher in a special school, Blackburn, 2010, p. 43)

Vulnerability at times of transition

Parents and educators share concern over the social and emotional vulnerability as CYP with FASDs move through the education system and into adult life.

> My argument is education has to be more than just about meeting the academic criteria and socially, she is just way behind her peers in mainstream school. She's 8 and she's just about learning to play with dolls and she doesn't really have imaginary play, she's so far behind socially but our education system doesn't see that as the main criterion.
>
> (Parent interview, Blackburn, 2010, p. 29)

- CYP with FASDs will continue to need provision and support throughout their adult life, which ideally include:
  - ongoing multi-disciplinary assessment leading to appropriate and sensitive support packages;
  - a commitment to maximising appropriate levels of independence;

---

1   The names of children have been changed to protect their identity.

- the provision of supported/sheltered living accommodation with access to assistance with daily living skills;
- supported work and leisure opportunities.
- Schools can support families in finding appropriate and suitable placement for CYP and providing information to future placement about how best to support CYP.

The overall implications for learning are that there is a necessity for extrinsic motivation to learn skills or complete tasks such as life skills, hygiene routines, and school-based tasks, particularly in secondary-aged children, requiring repetitive reminders and refocusing from adults. The amount of time CYP with FASDs spend engaged in learning tasks within the classroom in secondary-aged students can be as low as 40 per cent (Blackburn, 2010, p. 56). In addition, social communication difficulties mean that inappropriate interactions with others can leave CYP with FASDs vulnerable to bullying and other forms of abuse, or they may intimidate others with their overfriendly or overpowering behaviour.

These challenges can be compounded by other co-existing disorders, such as autistic spectrum disorders (ASDs) and attention deficit hyperactivity disorder (ADHD). Linked to this, many CYP will experience SPDs and may present with sensory-seeking behaviour such as inattention, hyperactivity, and distractibility. CYP's early family experiences may imply that attachment difficulties (ADs) are also a consideration for educators to be aware of, particularly where children have been placed in foster or adoptive families, as is most often the case for children with FASDs. The overlap between ASD and ADHD is discussed in Chapter 5, together with the classroom implications of those overlaps. A brief overview of SPDs and ADs is provided below. Mental health issues are also discussed.

Sensory processing disorders

Sensory processing disorders (SPDs) relate to the inability to use information received through the senses in order to function smoothly in daily life. SPDs is an umbrella term to cover a variety of neurological disabilities. Included in this are:

- Sensory modulation problems that pertain to how a child regulates his responses to sensations. This may result in a child being over-responsive (hypersensitive), under-responsive (hyposensitive), or sensory-seeking, and some children may fluctuate between these positions.
- Sensory discrimination difficulties that pertain to children who may have difficulty in distinguishing one sensation from another. We each have eight senses, including five external senses—visual, auditory, olfactory, tactile, and gustatory—and three internal—proprioceptive, vestibular, and organic. Each of these senses presents implications for the way we perceive and respond to our environment and perceive sensations such as pain, smell, taste, balance, and sound (see Appendix B).

- Sensory-based motor problems that relate to children who may position their body in unusual ways and have difficulty in conceiving of an action to do, planning how to organise and move their body, and carrying out the plan (Kranowitz, 2005, p. 13).

Sensory processing disorders can result in a range of symptoms from mild to severe, which can impact on interaction with others, functioning in daily life, the ability to learn, and general success throughout life. General strategies for including children and young people with SPDs in an educational setting are included in Chapter 4.

Attachment difficulties

Chapter 6 explains the role of secure attachments in family relationships. A solid and healthy attachment with a primary caregiver appears to be associated with a high probability of healthy relationships with others, whereas poor attachment with the mother or primary caregiver appears to be associated with a host of emotional and behavioural problems later in life (Perry, 2002). Studies have shown that children who have positive early attachment experiences do well as pre-school children (Sroufe, 1983, 1986), achieving high scores on ego-resilience and self esteem with less dependency on the educator and more positive affect towards the educator (p. 59). Securely attached CYP demonstrate a capacity to adapt to school and respond to the demands of academic and social settings in which learning takes place (Geddes, 2006, p. 47). Fundamentally, appropriate attachment with a primary caregiver is viewed as a foundation for optimal language, cognitive, and emotional development (Sparks and Gushurst, 1977), highlighting the interconnectedness between attachment and CYP's holistic development.

Children and young people's ability to adapt to a new caregiver is thought to be easier in the first six months of life than afterwards (Yarrow, 1964) and children under six months old are less rejecting and more accepting of new adoptive or foster parents than older infants (ibid.). However, the more caregivers a child is required to interact with, the more the ability to securely attach to others diminishes (Newton Verrier, 1993), which has implications for the attachment style of CYP who are exposed to multiple foster placements. In addition, there is a general feeling amongst clinicians working with CYP who are adopted that such children have the same issues whether they were adopted at birth or as teenagers. These issues relate to separation and loss, trust, rejection, guilt and shame, identity, intimacy, loyalty and mastery, or power and control (ibid., p. 7).

Infants develop a reflective sense of what others are likely to do in response to their own behaviour (Howe, 2005). This allows them to build mental representations or internal working models of expectations based on past experiences, allowing them to regulate the negative emotions of fear, distress, and anxiety when insecurity is felt. The formation of attachment relationships serves an important function as an emotional and physiological regulator for all humans as a social species (Chesney and Champion, 2008). Self regulation in CYP has been described as 'the developmental integration of emotion and cognition in early childhood' (Blair and Razza, 2007, p. 647) and has been found to account for variance in academic outcomes among three- to five-year-old children, indicating that success in self regulation helps prepare children for being successful in school (ibid.).

Thus, through the development of internal working models with sensitive attachment figures, CYP will begin to predict what might happen when feelings are expressed or needs displayed (ibid.). An internal working model of CYP's relationship with a caregiver will include concepts of:

- the self;
- others;
- expectations of the relationship and how the self and others are likely to behave and react.

The consistent availability of a sensitive caregiver in the development of a child's internal working model, therefore, is important as children begin to organise their attachment behaviour to increase the availability, proximity, and responsivity of their carers to meet their needs. The significance of a child's internal working model in relation to attachment and a positive sense of self is highlighted by Bowlby (1973, p. 208):

> A child who has experienced secure attachment is likely to . . . approach the world with confidence and, when faced with potentially alarming situations, is likely to tackle them effectively or to seek help in doing so.

Adverse experience of early attachment, such as inconsistency, unpredictability, or unavailability of a primary caregiver, that is not relieved by more positive relationships with others later on is 'very likely to have negative implications for both behaviour and learning' (Geddes, 2006, p. 48).

The early attachment experience of CYP, therefore, has implications for educators in supporting children's learning. It is important, therefore, that educators have an understanding of insecure attachment and the relationship between this and classroom behaviour.

There are three patterns/styles of insecure attachment identified by Ainsworth and colleagues (1978):

- organised attachment patterns:
  - the avoidant pattern;
  - the resistant/ambivalent pattern;
- disorganised attachment pattern.

Geddes (2006) outlines the broad implications of each of the insecure patterns/styles of attachment for classroom learning and CYP's relation with classroom environments, educators, and tasks with reference to a 'learning triangle'. For the CYP of a secure attachment, the balance of relationship between child, educator, and task reflects a fluid dynamic between engagement and support with the educator and involvement in the task (Figure 3.1).

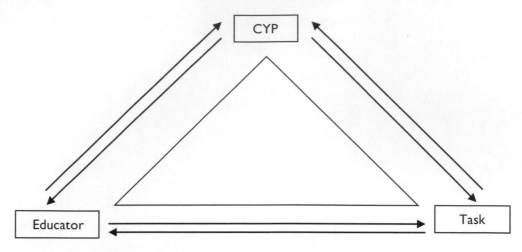

Figure 3.1 Learning triangle: secure attachment. Source: Geddes, 2006.

Table 3.2 Insecure attachment patterns: an overview of implications for classroom practice

	Attachment pattern/style		
	Avoidant	*Resistant/ambivalent*	*Disorganised/disorientated*
Approach to school/classroom	Apparent indifference to uncertainty in new situations	High level of anxiety and uncertainty	Intense anxiety which may be expressed as controlling and omnipotent
Response to educators	Denial of need for support and help from the educator	Need to hold on to the attention of the educator Apparent dependence on the educator in order to engage in learning Expressed hostility towards the educator when frustrated	Great difficulty experiencing trust in the authority of the educator but may submit to the authority of the head of the school May be unable to accept being taught, and/or unable to 'permit' the educator to know more than they do
Response to the task	Need to be autonomous and independent of the educator Hostility towards the educator is directed towards the task The task operates as an emotional safety barrier between the pupil and the educator	Difficulties attempting the task if unsupported Unable to focus on the task for fear of losing educator's attention	The task may seem like a challenge to their fears of incompetence, triggering overwhelming feelings of humiliation and rejection of the task Difficulty accepting 'not knowing' May wish to appear omnipotent and to know everything already
Skills and difficulties	Limited use of creativity Likely to be underachieving Limited use of language	Likely to be underachieving Language may be well developed but not consistent with levels of achievement Numeracy may be weak	May seem unimaginative and uncreative, and find conceptual thought difficult Likely to be underachieving and possibly at a very immature stage of learning

Source: Geddes, 2006.

As CYP mature they learn to be independent of the teacher and 'learn for themselves' (ibid., p. 59). For CYP with insecure attachment patterns/styles, a distorted version of the learning triangle is indicated, as outlined in Table 3.2.

Barrett and Trevitt (1991) identify the educator as the 'specific attachment person' in schools, particularly for anxious CYP. Educators can represent a 'secure base' in a school setting by providing sensitive, predictable responses to behaviour and learning needs for CYP with attachment difficulties.

Mental health

Children and young people with FASDs are at risk of developing secondary disabilities if sensitive and appropriate support packages are not received in their early years and primary education. One aspect of such disabilities is mental health problems. Mental health problems affect 30 to 40 per cent of all CYP at some time during childhood (Carpenter et al., 2010). The Mental Health Foundation estimates that 20 per cent of children up to the age of 16 years experience a mental health problem at some point during their development and 10 per cent present with a 'clinically recognisable' mental health disorder (including emotional disorders such as anxiety, phobias and depression, self harm and suicide, conduct disorders, hyperkinetic disorders, ASDs, psychotic disorders, eating disorders, and substance and drug abuse). Two per cent of children are diagnosed with two or more of these disorders (Office for National Statistics, 2004).

Among individuals affected by FASDs, the figure for the number affected by poor mental health rises to 87 per cent in adolescence and adult life, leading to the risk of suicide (23 per cent) (Streissguth and Kanter, 1997). Mental health problems can have a significant effect on engagement with the curriculum and learning. If a child is depressed, for example, this impacts on their enthusiasm for learning and socialising and their ability to pay attention and access memories or allocate sufficient resources to tasks because they are distracted by negative thoughts (Ellis and Ashbrook, 1988). Generally CYP who are depressed engage less effectively than those who are not depressed (Cooper and Tiknaz, 2007). Anxious CYP, on the other hand, may display a range of attention problems, such as narrow attention span and distractibility. Anxiety and worry can have a negative impact on information processing, motivation, and memory (Eysenck and Calvo, 1992; Eysenck and Keane, 1995). Educators supporting CYP with FASDs, therefore, will need to be aware of mental health issues, how these may manifest in children, and how best to support a child with organic brain damage and compounding mental health difficulties, so that they can 'lift children and young people from vulnerability to positions of resilience' (Carpenter et al., 2010, p. 1).

Transdisciplinary practice

Educators and the professionals who support CYP with FASDs in the classroom will require an understanding of the compounding factors associated with the condition, and ensure

Table 3.3 An overview of professionals involved in the support needs of children and young people with FASD

Education/therapies supporting within school	Medical/health	Social care/charity
• Educational psychologist • Physiotherapist • Local authority inclusion support team • Music therapist • Play therapist • Learning disabilities team • Occupational therapist • Speech and language therapist	• Dietitian • Geneticist • Mental health team • FASD specialist • Orthoptics • Psychologist • Psychiatrist • General practitioner • Orthopaedic spinal specialist • Paediatrician	• Social care professionals • Police officers • Children's charities (NSPCC, Barnardo's) • Charities related to FASDs (NOFAS-UK, FASDTrust, FASAware)

Source: Blackburn, 2010.

continuing multi-disciplinary assessment that is necessary to allow identification of secondary disabilities so that proactive action can be taken to ameliorate the effects. The importance of working closely with families and 'putting families at the centre' of their child's educational journey (Braybrook, personal communication, 2010) in these circumstances cannot be overestimated.

Chapter 4 outlines approaches that will assist educators in designing appropriate curricula for CYP with FASDs. In order to effectively support these CYP, educators will need to engage with a range of professionals, which may typically include those listed in Table 3.3.

It is important that educators be aware of the role that each of these professionals can take in the education and support needs of CYP with FASDs in order to optimise the learning opportunities provided by their involvement in the design and delivery of personalised curricula and engage with them fully. For a full discussion relating to transdisciplinary practice and practical examples of exemplary collaborative practice in transdisciplinary teams for children with FASDs, particularly those with complex needs, see Carpenter and colleagues (2011, pp. 146–153).

References

Ainsworth, M.D.S., Blehar, M., Waters, E., and Wall, S. (1978) *Patterns of Attachment: A Psychological Study of the Strange Situation.* Hillsdale, NJ: Erlbaum.

Barrett, M. and Trevitt, J. (1991) *Attachment Behaviour and the Schoolchild.* London: Routledge.

Blair, C. and Razza, R.P. (2007) 'Relating effortful control, executive function, and false belief understanding to emerging math and literacy ability in kindergarten'. *Child Development*, 78: 647–663.

Blackburn, C. (2010) *Facing the Challenge and Shaping the Future for Students with Foetal Alcohol Spectrum Disorders* (FAS-eD Project). London: National Organisation on Fetal Alcohol Syndrome (UK).

Blackburn, C., Carpenter, B., and Egerton, J. (2009) 'Facing the Challenge and Shaping the Future for Students with Foetal Alcohol Spectrum Disorders' (FAS-eD Project) Literature Review. London: National Organisation on Fetal Alcohol Syndrome (UK).

Blaschke, K., Mataverne, M., and Struck, J. (2009) *Fetal Alcohol Spectrum Disorders Education Strategies: Working with Students with a Fetal Alcohol Spectrum Disorder in the Education System*. University of South Dakota: Sandford School of Medicine.

Bowlby, J. (1973) *Attachment and Loss. Vol. 2 Separation: Anxiety and Anger*. London: Hogarth Press.

Carpenter, B., Coughlan, B., and Fotheringham, J. (2010) *Mental Health and Emotional Well-Being: The New Dimension in the Curriculum for Children and Young People with Special Educational Needs*. Complex Needs Series No.4. London: Specialist Schools and Academies Trust (SSAT).

Carpenter, B., Egerton, J., Brooks, T., Cockbill, B., Fotheringham, J., and Rawson, H. (2011) *The Complex Learning Difficulties and Disabilities Research Project: Developing Meaningful Pathways to Personalised Learning Final Report*. London: Specialist Schools and Academies Trust (SSAT).

Chesney, A.R. and Champion, P. (2008) 'Understanding the dynamics between preterm infants and their families'. *Support for Learning*, 23 (3): 144–151.

Cooper, P. and Tiknaz, Y. (2007) *Nurture Groups in School and at Home: Connecting with Children with Social, Emotional and Behavioural Difficulties*. London: Jessica Kingsley.

Ellis, H.C. and Ashbrook, P.W. (1988) 'Resource allocation model of the effects of depressed mood states on memory', in Fielder, K. and Forgas, J. (eds) *Affect, Cognition, and Social Behaviour*. Toronto: Hogrefe.

Eysenck, M.W. and Calvo, M.G. (1992) 'Anxiety and peformance: the processing efficiency theory'. *Cognition and Emotion*, 6: 409–434.

Eysenck, M.W. and Keane, M.T. (1995) *Cognitive Psychology: A Student's Handbook*. Hove, East Sussex: Psychology Press.

Geddes, H. (2006) *Attachment in the Classroom: The Links between Children's Early Experience, Emotional Well-Being and Performance in School*. London: Worth Publishing.

Howe, D. (2005) *Child Abuse and Neglect: Attachment, Development and Intervention*. Basingstoke, Hampshire: Palgrave Macmillan.

Kellerman, T. (2008) *Prenatal Alcohol Exposure and the Brain*. NIAAA Publications. Online at: www.come-over.to/FAS/FASbrain.htm, accessed 20 January 2012.

Kranowitz, C.S. (2005) *The Out of Sync Child: Recognizing and Coping with Sensory Processing Disorder*. London: Penguin Group.

Newton Verrier, N. (1993) *The Primal Wound: Understanding the Adopted Child*. Baltimore, MD: Gateway Press.

Office for National Statistics (2004) *News Release: One in Ten Children has a Mental Disorder*. Online at: http://medvctande.dk/OneOfTen_MentalDisorderUK.pdf, accessed 26 January 2012.

Perry, B. (2002) 'Childhood experience and the expression of genetic potential: what childhood neglect tells us about nature and nurture', *Brain and Mind*, 3: 79–100.

Sparks, S.N. and Gushurst, C. (1977) 'Interactions of neonates and infants with prenatal cocaine exposure', in Rossetti, L.M. and Kile, J.E. (eds) *Early Intervention for Special Populations of Infants and Toddlers*. San Diego: Singular Publishing Group.

Sroufe, A. (1986) 'Appraisal: Bowlby's contribution to psychoanalytic theory and developmental psychology; attachment: separation: loss', *Journal of Child Psychology and Psychiatry*, 27 (6): 841–849.

Sroufe, L.A. (1983) 'Infant–caregiver attachment patterns of adaptation in pre-school: the roots of maladaptation and competence', in Permutter, M. (ed.) *Minnesota Symposium of Child Psychology: Vol. 16*. Hillsdale, NJ: Erlbaum, pp. 41–81.

Streissguth, A.P. and Kanter, J. (eds) (1997) *The Challenges of Foetal Alcohol Syndrome: Overcoming Secondary Disabilities*. Seattle, WA: University of Washington Press:

Yarrow, L.J. (1964) 'Separation from parents during early childhood', in Hoffman, M.L. and Hoffman, L.W. (eds) *Review of Child Development Research*. New York: Russel Sage Foundation.

A teaching and learning framework to support children and young people with fetal alcohol spectrum disorders

Including children and young people (CYP) with fetal alcohol spectrum disorders (FASDs) in any educational setting presents challenges as well as opportunities for educators. As outlined in Chapter 3, CYP with FASDs have practical strengths which provide the opportunity to plan curricula and tasks around the CYP's interests and motivators. Challenges are posed for educators in relation to the uneven learning profile of CYP with FASDs, their social and emotional vulnerability, and their sometimes hidden difficulties.

This chapter presents a framework of teaching and learning strategies which have been compiled and trialled with educators and other professionals supporting CYP with FASDs and their families in mainstream and special schools in the UK and are therefore evidence-based (see Blackburn, 2010; Carpenter, 2011). They have also been reviewed by speech and language therapists and an occupational therapist. The strategies suggested are also influenced and supported by international research and guidelines (see Kleinfeld and Westcott, 1993; Steissguth and Kanter, 1997; Kleinfeld *et al.*, 2000; Clarren, 2004).

These strategies may include ideas which some schools are already aware of and are using as part of their inclusive practice. In addition, some ideas may appear to be suitable for a particular age group. It is important to remember that there is a wide variation of developmental age and ability amongst CYP with FASDs of all ages. Some schools may be aware of some of these strategies but have not used them with CYP with FASDs. It is hoped that the framework will be useful to a range of educators including early childhood educators, teaching assistants, learning mentors, trainee teachers, newly qualified teachers, more experienced teachers, Special Educational Needs Co-ordinators (SENCo), curriculum leaders, school leaders, educational advisors, and any of the professionals responsible for supporting educators. The range of strategies offered in this chapter, therefore, is designed to reflect a wide scope of knowledge and confidence in supporting CYP with FASDs. The strategies are linked not to curricula but to developmental domains. It is important to remember that these domains are inter-related and that child development should be considered holistically. In particular, the links between cognitive, communication, and emotional development are important to observe as CYP with FASDs will usually need support in one or more of these domains.

The strategies are designed not to be prescriptive, but rather to represent a collection of ideas and interventions to use as a starting point to allow educators to develop their own personalised curricula for CYP with FASDs.

One way to use the framework is to decide which barrier to learning is causing difficulty for the child in question and to try one new strategy at a time, record the outcome (whether it worked and, if it did not work, reflect on why that might be: does it need adapting, a different approach, or a different environment, etc.?), record the benefit to the child, and ensure that the strategy is shared with other members of staff and professionals, and, in particular, parents, before focusing on the next barrier to learning. Useful tools to assist with this, including an observation sheet and an inquiry framework for learning, can be found on the Complex Learning Difficulties and Disabilities Research Project website (http://complexld.ssatrust.org.uk/project-information.html). Schools may also have their own observation tools for recording the engagement, learning, and progress of CYP with FASDs against curriculum goals and individual targets. The emphasis should be on reflective practice using this text as a guide for reflection, so that educators consider the environment, tasks, curricula, and opportunities they offer to CYP with FASDs based on their neurodevelopmental, physical, social and emotional, and communication needs.

Personalising learning

The hallmarks of personalised learning are ambitious objectives, challenging personal targets, rapid intervention to keep pupils on trajectory, and vigorous assessment to check and maintain progress. Within this there are clear plans to support those CYP who do not or cannot maintain trajectory (DCSF, 2007, p. 64). McPhillips and colleagues (2010) highlight the importance of educators' appreciation of 'neurodiversity' in the classroom, pointing to the need for an increased awareness of the scientific basis of biological diversity and how it relates to the needs of CYP. This invites schools to personalise learning (ibid.) for CYP by encouraging teachers to appreciate the individual learning needs and styles of CYP and match the environment, learning task, and interaction between CYP and instruction and task, to both the learning profile and the learning style. For example, as already stated, CYP with FASDs have difficulties with abstract concepts, time, money, relationships, and key life skills. However, they have practical strengths and abilities and learn well through visual–kinaesthetic approaches.

Children and young people with FASDs can experience low levels of behavioural, cognitive, and emotional engagement in school (see Blackburn, 2010). Personalising learning can provide educators with a platform for involving and engaging CYP with FASDs through curriculum calibration (Carpenter *et al.*, 2011) and inquiry-based approaches (see Chapter 5).

Establishing children's strengths and interests

As stated, CYP with FASDs often have strengths in practical areas such as individual sports, the arts, and languages. Information can be gathered from classroom observations (which will ideally include video observation so that class teams can discuss observations together), discussions with families and other professionals supporting the child both within school and externally, and discussions with the child him/herself.

The Strengths and Difficulties Questionnaire (SDQ) (see www.sdqinfo.com) is a brief behavioural screening questionnaire for use with CYP aged 3–16 years. It exists in several versions to meet the needs of researchers, clinicians, and educationalists, and CYP's strengths and difficulties are scored against the following components:

- emotional symptoms;
- conduct problems;
- hyperactivity/inattention;
- peer relationship problems;
- prosocial behaviour.

The questionnaire can be answered by parents, educators (and other professionals), and CYP, according to their chronological and developmental age. The results can be used to indicate strengths and difficulties in the above areas and to inform future assessments. For example, if a child is thought to be displaying conduct problems, but both parent and educator SDQ completion indicate hyperactivity, this could highlight an overlooked aspect of the child's learning profile and lead to further assessment and specific interventions to address hyperactivity. One study indicated that CYP with FASDs show needs in all of the above areas, with the highest scores being presented in those in secondary education. Prosocial behaviour can be a strength for CYP with FASDs, highlighting their very friendly nature (Blackburn, 2010). Carmichael and colleagues (1977) found that *young* children with FASDs in particular are socially engaging, interested in others, very talkative, and affectionate.

An engagement approach to assessing and supporting CYP's learning needs can be found on the Complex Learning Difficulties and Disabilities (CLDD) Research Project website and is discussed in Chapter 5 of this book.

Liaising with families

Families' experiences will be an important aspect of assessing how a child is able to cope in new and unusual situations, and sharing information with them about curriculum content and approaches will be key to providing consistency and routine for CYP with FASDs . This will help to reduce anxiety and worry for both children and parents (see Chapter 6).

Cognitive and communication development

Children and young people with FASDs characteristically experience developmental delays, which impact on engagement within the classroom and progress within the curriculum.

Inattention, hyperactivity, and distractibility (often due to sensory processing difficulties) in the classroom interfere with engagement with the curriculum, particularly in secondary education (see Chapter 3). Their difficulties epitomise that much-used phrase 'complex needs' (Carpenter, 2011). Equal and appropriate peer interaction is difficult across the age and curriculum range, as CYP with FASDs often prefer the company of younger children and irritate peers with their overfriendly approach to relationships. Medical issues may cause irregular or patchy attendance at school, and attachment difficulties may impact upon relationships with adults and peers. For children with sensory processing disorders (SPDs), the learning environment may need careful consideration in order to enhance their ability to concentrate and process information.

The challenge for educators is to recognise and identify the developmental level at which the child with an FASD is operating, and provide appropriate support for development and progress across the curriculum.

Case study 1: cognitive and communication development

Molly (age eight years) listens well in the classroom and enjoys school. She wants to do well and be included and is willing to learn. Her enthusiasm is coupled with a visual impairment, small stature, immaturity, and inattention as well as learning difficulties. This has implications for where she is able to sit in the classroom in order to see the teacher and whiteboard, how her peers treat her in equality terms, her ability to stay on task and retain information, and the length of time she is able to focus.

For example, there is a temptation for peers to 'baby' her as it is not always easy for her to follow the rules of playground games or play with them on an equal basis. Her lack of focus and attention means that tasks must necessarily be broken down into small steps and highly personalised to her individual needs in order to engage her in learning. Her visual impairment means that she must sit near the front of the classroom so that she is able to see the teacher and whiteboard, and also has implications for the use of computers and visual equipment in ICT.

Including this child in a mainstream secondary setting and providing access to the National Curriculum have been possible through a combination of adult support and scaffolding, personalised teaching and learning, and partnership with parents. For example:

- Abstract concepts such as money are taught using a range of concrete examples such as oversized laminated pictures of coins, plastic coins, and games to accommodate her visual impairment. The equipment is then sent home so that Molly can practise with parents. This is then reinforced with a trip to the shop to use real money and facilitate the transfer of knowledge from the classroom situation to a real-life practical application with peer and adult support.

- Life skills such as cooking, hygiene, peer relations, emotions, safety, and life cycle issues are taught through attendance at a weekly life skills class with peers.
- Recording of achievement is appropriate to the situation. For example, photographs of Molly taken at various stages of the learning process demonstrate progress, without the need for her to undertake lengthy writing activities, which tire and frustrate her, leading to a sense of failure and low self esteem.
- Pictures and symbols are displayed below the whiteboard so that she and other children with additional needs have a visible timetable of the day/lesson. The teacher/ inclusion support assistant will talk through the timetable so that the children know what is happening now and next.
- A buddy system is provided at break and lunch times to ensure that Molly has peer companionship and support throughout the day. A home-link diary is used to keep Molly's parents informed, and they are able to use this to ensure that the school is aware of issues at home that may impact on Molly's learning or emotional well being throughout the school day.

Strategies to support cognitive and communication development

Figure 4.1 This six-year-old attends a special school where a total communication approach is used throughout the school, including the use of gesture, sign language, visual timetables, and other visual communication systems to support the development of communication skills.

Table 4.1 Teaching strategies to support cognitive and communication development

Communication	• Provide opportunities for small group work. This will provide a secure environment in which the CYP may feel more confident to ask and respond to questions than they would in large group situations • Break instructions into chunks. Keep instructions as short as possible, provide them one at a time, and reinforce with visual cues as prompts • Break tasks into small achievable steps starting with what you know the child can already do to in order to build self esteem • Provide tactile examples of what you are teaching. Allowing the child with an FASD to touch, see, and/or feel something will help him/her to succeed in learning what you are teaching. This can be particularly helpful for practical sessions such as science, where the need to touch and feel objects can lead to dangerous situations. Providing a one-to-one session with the child before the lesson, in order to enable safety messages to be understood, can reduce impulsivity and increase safety • Use the child's own life when teaching new ideas. This will give the child a reference point for their learning • Provide visual aids (such as pictures, symbols, and timetables) to reinforce instructions and tasks (see example in Chapter 5) • Make visual timetables concrete by including photographs of the child doing activities, rather than symbols or drawings • Use consistent language throughout the school. For the child with more complex communication needs, formal signing and other forms of assistive and augmentative communication may be necessary • Use positive language; tell the child what you would like them to do rather than what you would not like them to do • Avoid confusion by being direct: instead of saying 'Do you know where your lunch box is?', say 'Where is your lunch box?' • Identify key words/concepts for a topic and discuss with the child before the topic is introduced to the whole class (pretutoring)[a] • Language used in the classroom will ideally reflect the language used in tests and exams to avoid confusion
Literacy skills	• If the child difficulty with learning to read through a phonic approach encourage them to build up a sight vocabulary by using a multi-sensory approach such as Look, Cover, Write, Check. Expect to repeat words frequently • The ability to build a story by sequencing symbols and pictures is a simple way to build confidence. Encourage parents to write events from the weekend in the child's home–school diary so that the child can be supported to remember events they may have forgotten and record them with adult support through the use of symbols and pictures • Encourage the enjoyment of books at a level that is developmentally appropriate to the child; picture books without too much text may be more appealing regardless of age • Provide the child with a reading journal where they can record their reading at school and home. Ensure that reading targets are broken down into achievable steps (perhaps two to three pages). Provide two or three comprehension questions for them to answer about the text • If the child has difficulty with directionality of text use coloured dots (green for left and red for right) to indicate the correct direction. Explain that we start at green and stop at red • Allow opportunities to tell or record stories pictorially as the child may not be ready for lengthy writing • Consider colour coding words for sentence construction. For example, all nouns could be red, all verbs yellow and adjectives green (taking into account the child's own colour preferences). This works well when used with writing frames • Use picture dictionaries where possible to aid vocabulary development • Provide audiotapes or CDs of textbooks, literature, and social stories • Provide a laptop and/or scribe if necessary for written work. This can help to improve enjoyment of a task and improve concentration and engagement with a task

Literacy skills	• Mind maps can be used to help organise thoughts and tasks and help to embed understanding of subjects and tasks • Writing frames can be used for written homework, providing clear structure and concise organisation of what to put on the page and where, making tasks more manageable • Consider other methods of recording progress such as photographs and video/audio recording for CYP who find lengthy writing tasks difficult
Abstract concepts (including mathematics)	• Demonstrate a concept, show rather than tell, and be prepared to repeat the demonstration/instruction • Provide concrete examples of abstract concepts such as number lines, abacus for understanding place value, and real objects for counting in sequence and establishing the concept of what numbers stand for • Use art projects to make abstract concepts more concrete. Use coloured sand to teach the student about volume. Give the child a clear plastic cup or a clean glass jar and allow him/her to fill in the item with different colours of sand • Use ICT as a visual representation of number rules and mathematical concepts. Computer-based learning programmes may work well because they are repetitive and visual and provide immediate feedback coupled with a hands-on learning experience • Teach cause and effect with the use of three-dimensional tactile resources, such as pop-up toys, scented bubbles, jigsaws, and books with sound effects • Use vertical number lines instead of horizontal number lines so that the child can identify that adding results in numbers going up and subtracting results in numbers going down, in a visual way • When teaching the child about temperature, use a blanket as an example of cold and hot. The child will understand that they will put on a blanket when they are cold and will take the blanket off when they are warm • Plan games activities involving right and left instructions • Plan physical activities involving mathematical concepts such as number, positional language, colour and shape, as movement can aid memory retention • Use a consistent language for all concepts and in all classrooms/lessons; for example, do not say 'nought' one day and 'zero' the next • Too many maths problems/questions on one page may overwhelm the child. One or two problems/questions on one page with plenty of white space in between is more manageable • Include the child's name in word problems • Produce mathematical process cards by highlighting examples of mathematical processes (e.g. multiplication, division, and subtraction) broken down in a step-by-step process for the child to refer to as a reminder • Avoid mixing addition and subtraction, multiplication, and division problems on the same page. Ensure that the operation symbol is in large and in bold type so that it is clear what the child is expected to do • Questions and problems involving a story that needs decoding is an extra task, which may be overwhelming. Allow extra time and provide adult support • Graph or lined paper can help the child to line mathematical problems up more easily than plain paper • Expect learning to take place at a slower pace, make teaching interactive, and allow the child to talk through mathematical processes and problems as this may help with memory
Money/time	• Use real money and clock faces as they are more concrete and this will allow the child to move the hands on the clock • Consider the use of a digital clock if the child finds conventional clock faces difficult • Use objects in the classroom and around the school such as calendars, clocks, and watches to highlight numbers and number patterns to encourage the ability to generalise • Plan role play sessions involving time and money with shop, restaurant and shopping scenarios. Use real objects so that the child builds a stronger association with real life scenarios, and does not become confused by unnecessary substitutions which they may not link with reality

Table 4.1 (continued)

Money/time	• Use sand timers, egg timers, growing plants, and daily calendars to help the child to visualise the passing of time • Use timers to help the child to recognise how long they have to complete a task
Number sense	• Relate numbers to meaningful concrete objects to enable the child to view numbers as values rather than labels. For example, there are two wheels on a bicycle, three wheels on a tricycle, and four wheels on a car • Create a large number line across the classroom which the child can physically move along • Help the child to recognise that many things cannot be measured precisely, by providing practice with estimation in a range of situations • Provide a range of materials that involve number and number representations such as dice, dominoes, playing cards, coins, clocks, and rulers • Look for ways to incorporate the the child's own interests and strengths into number work in order to personalise their learning. For example, football teams provide countless opportunities for number work
Memory/ organisation/ following rules	• Consider whether non-compliance with rules is due to lack of understanding or because the child has been distracted • Provide clear, consistently applied rules across the school to reduce the number of things that need to be remembered • Expect to repeat instructions and rules frequently • Ensure that the consequences of not following rules are consistently applied. This will ensure that the child is more aware of his/her own actions and helps students to make better decisions • Use short sentences in instructions and lesson delivery to reduce complexity • Allow extra time for the child to process information. This will help to reduce anxiety, which is known to cause more problems for CYP with FASDs and can result in outbursts, lack of engagement with a task/subject, and poor self esteem • Using an animated voice, facial expressions and exaggerated gestures will engage the child, who is developmentally younger, and aid memory retention • Provide concrete examples of abstract concepts to aid retention • Provide visual timetables in classrooms as a memory aid and to enable the child to see what is happening now and next • Visual timetables would ideally use photographs of the child as a concrete representation of what is required and what is happening next • Check the child's understanding of instructions and tasks frequently, particularly in relation to homework • When asking a child to repeat an instruction you have given, ask them to repeat it in their own words to ensure that they have processed and understood the information • Communicate regularly with parents/carers about homework through a home–school diary or emails • Use appropriate reward systems that reward the child for their individual achievement and which motivate them personally
Sensory processing difficulties (may present as behaviour difficulties such as hyperactivity, impulsivity, inattention, distractibility)	• Consider asking an occupational therapist to undertake a sensory profile if the child seems switched off frequently, or easily overwhelmed by texture, noise, light, smell, movement, sound, temperature, crowded places, or too much dialogue, as they may be hyposensitive or hypersensitive • Consider if diet is a contributing factor or if there are any underlying undetected health problems • Remove as many distractions from the learning environment as possible • Seat the child in the same place consistently, ideally where the teacher can easily see the child (and vice versa) and maintain eye contact (some children will be better placed near the front and others may need to be at the back where they can see everyone and leave the room quickly if necessary). Ensure that all staff in contact with the child are aware of the issues relating to sensory processing difficulties and the impact on learning

| Sensory processing difficulties (may present as behaviour difficulties such as hyperactivity, impulsivity, inattention, distractibility) | • Consider the classroom and school environment in terms of noise, light, sound, and ease of access. Particularly problematic are fluorescent lights, scraping chairs, air conditioning units, school bells, ticking clocks, echo in changing rooms and toilets, chemicals and Bunsen burners in practical lessons, textiles in technology lessons, some food items, and perfume aromas
• Provide a room that represents a calmer environment than a classroom and the opportunity to visit this when the child becomes overwhelmed. Provide earphones, eye masks, lavender,[b] and calming music. If appropriate, provide earphones to use in the classroom
• Place carpet or tennis balls on the legs of tables and chairs to eliminate noise when other children move
• Seat the child as far as possible from distractions such as windows, doors, and the movement of other students
• Consider colour/shape coding items that the child needs to access frequently, for example red triangles for maths books or yellow circles for literacy books
• Frame the child's working area (including seat and desk) with masking tape to keep their attention focused on their work space and enable them to remember their personal space
• For carpet work, provide an individual cushion for the child to remind them of their personal space
• Provide a stress ball or other item to encourage focus
• Keep tasks short and achievable and break them up with physical activity to expend energy and refocus attention
• Gradually build up the time that the child is expected to sustain attention. Make a visual chart showing progress with tasks to share with them so that they can see their own achievement in terms of sustained attention
• Allow the child to leave the classroom earlier or later than peers in order to avoid noisy/busy corridors when moving from one classroom to another
• Allow the child to enter and leave the snack and lunchtime facilities before or after peers in order to avoid queues and crowds
• Use percussion instructions for the child to create rhythms and to practise following instructions to play and copy patterns. The child will need to listen and sustain attention to hear patterns
• Music therapy sessions can provide a safe space for the child to explore and express emotions and feelings, reducing anxiety and hyperactivity. This can also improve listening and attention skills |

Notes

a   Pretutoring is the direct and specific teaching of key language before it is introduced to the rest of the class using oral, not written, interaction. It is used to introduce topic work, stories, and poems to pupils who have language learning difficulties. Pretutoring key language gives pupils the chance to learn the meaning of words, and to practise using them so, when the words occur in the class lesson later, they have some understanding (Birmingham City Council, 2004).

b   Care must be taken with CYP who have epilepsy as certain smells may trigger this, and lavender is one of them.

Brooks (2010), in her work on learning environments for students with autistic spectrum disorder (ASDs), highlights the importance of recognising the impact that sensory processing difficulties can have on CYP's ability to engage and learn, and adapting the environment to accommodate CYP's sensory processing needs. It is important to realise that sensory processing difficulties may present differently in individual children. Nevertheless, Brooks recommends some general considerations, including building design, lighting, flooring, colour and layout of furniture, equipment and seating, as well as the use of sensory integration equipment, such as swings and rocking chairs, to support vestibular and proprioceptive sensory needs.

She clarifies this further by suggesting that teachers accommodate exteroceptive sensory processing difficulties through providing a *low arousal physical environment* characterised by solid neutral colours, non-reflective surfaces, sound insulation, curvilinear design, distraction-free, uncluttered, anti-tilt chairs, separate rooms for noise/quiet, separate storage spaces, suitable artificial and natural lighting, and blinds. In addition, sensory regulatory difficulties should be accommodated through providing suitable areas/opportunities/activities for *physical exercise and sensory regulatory activities* such as rocking/swinging (ibid., p. 292).

Appendix A presents the location and function of the seven senses, along with examples of behaviours resulting from hyper/hyposensitivity in each sense (see also Chapter 3).

Strategies to support CYP with attachment difficulties

Schools provide an opportunity to provide a secure base for CYP with attachment difficulties, enabling them to function effectively both emotionally and cognitively. Geddes (2006, p. 140) recommends that the following be incorporated into everyday practice to facilitate this:

- respect for all CYP no matter what their skills and difficulties;
- a building which is safe and adequately supervised;
- sensitivity to the meaning of communications implied by the behaviour of children and empathy for what the child may be attempting to convey;
- predictable, reliable routines;
- a fast response to absence – noticing the absent pupil;
- consistent rules and expectations framed around keeping pupils, staff, and the building safe;
- familiar long-term relationships so that children feel 'known';
- modelling of good relationships between adults;
- informed reflection about incidents rather than reactivity;
- a system of disciplinary procedures which is fair to all.

Behaviour development

Children and young people with FASDs often lack inhibition, interact inappropriately with adults and peers, and fail to understand cause and effect and consequences of actions. They may experience multiple foster and/or adoption placement throughout their lives (see Chapter 3). This can result in their forming indiscriminate and/or inappropriate interaction patterns with others, including being exploited or bullied, putting themselves and others in dangerous situations, and being prone to substance misuse. They can be impulsive and overexcited, which can put them and others in danger. The implications are that CYP with FASDs sometimes come to the attention of the criminal justice system for criminal offences.

Educators can help by recognising that these CYP need additional support to form appropriate relationships, understand rules, and learn valuable life skills. CYP with FASDs may need close adult supervision throughout the day (and throughout their lives) to ensure their safety and the safety of others.

Case study 2: behaviour development

Jane is 13 years old. She is a keen learner, and when she is confident she can complete tasks. She enjoys school and in particular she likes public speaking, drama, French, history, literacy, dance, and gymnastics. She takes pride in her artistic talent and her ability to write stories. She is noted for her general knowledge and politeness.

This enthusiasm is coupled with extreme impulsivity, hyperactivity, and a propensity to become overstimulated by busy, noisy, tactile environments (due to an SPD). This has particular implications for practical lessons such as science, food technology, and physical education, where close supervision is required to ensure her safety and the safety of other students and staff. For example, in science lessons, she can easily become overwhelmed by equipment such as Bunsen burners, bright liquids, and noisy experiments. When she is overstimulated, she may pick up or touch equipment (Bunsen burners, ovens, chemicals) and move around the room with them before a member of staff can react. When in noisy changing rooms, overstimulation can lead to her climbing on top of equipment such as lockers.

Including this child in a mainstream secondary setting and providing access to the National Curriculum have been possible through a combination of careful and thorough risk assessments, adult support and scaffolding, personalised teaching and learning, and partnership with parents.

For example:

- Before practical sessions such as food technology or science take place, the science teacher or autistic spectrum condition (ASC) unit teacher (accompanied by a teaching assistant) will walk and talk the student through the equipment, providing her with clear demonstrations and explanations of the safe use of equipment. Jane is then in a position to attend a lesson alongside her peers armed with a basic understanding of the principles and expectations. This will always be supported by at least one-to-one and sometimes two-to-one adult supervision.
- Jane has a visual timetable located in the ASC unit, which she looks at each morning on arrival at the unit.
- A smaller version of the timetable is copied into her individual planner so that she can view it during lessons as necessary.
- Teaching assistants monitor her anxiety and arousal level throughout the day

through discussions with her and liaise with her and each other, as well as the ASC unit teacher, about those lessons where more support may be necessary. They can then discuss the nature of support necessary to ameliorate the effects of her sensory processing difficulties as far as possible.

- The ASC unit teacher (and school SENCo when appropriate) corresponds daily with Jane's parents by email regarding issues arising.

In addition, Jane is provided with access to occupational therapy and music therapy to address sensory processing and social and emotional difficulties, combining a therapeutic approach with a differentiated national curriculum.

Strategies to support behaviour development

Figure 4.2 This 13-year-old attends an autistic spectrum condition (ASC) unit attached to a mainstream secondary school. Most of her learning takes place in mainstream classes with some individual programmes being delivered in the ASC unit. She is also supported by an occupational therapist and a music therapist within the school.

Table 4.2 Teaching strategies to support behaviour development

Understanding danger (including stranger danger)	• Conduct a safety walk around the school buildings and grounds with the child in order to highlight dangers around school • Provide a safe environment and ensure adequate adult support • Provide safety notices and ensure appropriate explanation at a level of understanding appropriate to the child • Liaise with parents/agencies/pupil to identify danger issues. (Agencies such as Barnardo's can work alongside teaching assistants in small groups with students, providing a safe environment for students to express concerns and ask questions confidently) • Ensure effective communication with parents and cascade information from parents to all staff • Explain steps for keeping safe with constant and frequent reminders and reinforcement. This should include modelling safe procedures by staff with explanations of how to stay safe • The provision of a very safe learning environment can mean that there is little need for children to be wary of strangers. Provide opportunities to meet strangers through organised visits and through visitors to the school in order to build awareness of risks whilst working on strategies to avoid or remove them. Address stranger danger and personal safety issues during circle time/drama work
Impulsivity/ lack of inhibition	• Provide constant supervision and appropriate adult ratios in practical lessons and laboratory situations (it may be necessary for two-to-one adult supervision during some practical lessons to support unusual levels of impulsivity/hyperactivity) • Provide specific teaching of routines and safety rules • Be prepared to repeat instructions/routines/rules as often as necessary to ensure understanding. This will help to increase confidence and motivation • Provide a quiet space to discuss sensitive issues with the student • Where changes to timetables and schedules are necessary ensure that the student is informed as soon as possible and given an appropriate explanation. This will help to reduce anxiety and disruptive behaviour • Provide adult support to prepare the student for and guide them through changes to timetables and arrangements • Provide a quiet time area where the student can go to calm down. Provide earphones, eye masks, lavender,[a] and calming music. Ensure that this is viewed by the student as a positive aid for them to regulate their own emotions in order to build confidence and self esteem • Provide visual prompts showing required behaviour, preferably using photographs of the child rather than pictures or symbols • Record the occurrence of incidents in order to identify possible triggers that may be causing distress. Monitor to see if incidents occur at particular times, with particular peers or members of staff, and so on, and make adaptations in order to reduce occurrences

Note
a   Care must be taken with CYP who have epilepsy as certain smells may trigger this, and lavender is one of them.

Social and emotional development

For CYP with FASDs, developing age-appropriate, mutually beneficial, and reciprocal relationships can be a challenge because of their lack of understanding about social cues and difficulties with theory of mind. Memory deficits make understanding cause and effect and consequences of actions difficult to grasp. Coming into contact with the criminal justice system, disrupted schooling, and social isolation are common features of adolescents with FASDs, if these difficulties are not identified early and appropriate and effective support provided.

The challenge for educators is to monitor friendships and activities in and out of school which may adversely influence the individual with an FASD to become involved in inappropriate relationships or activities. A key worker or learning mentor can provide a guiding voice in leading CYP with FASDs through the maze of changes to emotions and feelings as well as body changes in adolescence and at key transition stages. Educators can take a leading part in educating the wider community about the difficulties that individuals with FASDs may face in everyday life so that an inclusive society is available for those affected.

Case study 3: social and emotional development

Chris (age 19 years) is enthusiastic to be involved in school life, is keen to help others and enjoys reading, sport, and anything physical or practical such as food technology and art. He also enjoys joint work when the class works together to produce a piece of writing. However, his inability to stay on task for longer than 15 minutes at a time can be a barrier to learning, particularly within numeracy.

Chris has social communication difficulties. This can mean that he can be overpowering in his relationship with others, which can be a barrier to forming friendships. In addition, this can cause difficulties for Chris in the area of inappropriate interactions with others. This has already resulted in one night in legal custody. His inability to understand 'appropriateness' in social communications has implications for work experience as well as supervision within the school environment, necessitating one-to-one supervision 100 per cent of the time in order to protect him and other vulnerable young people.

In order to provide work placements for this student, it has been necessary for the school to think about placements within the school and, when considering external work placements or interactions in the community, be able to provide one-to-one adult supervision. In addition, small group and class work has focused on interactions with others, bullying, and appropriate behaviour in order to prepare Chris for life, both within his community and in future employment, facilitating his success in making a positive contribution as well as achieving economic well being.

Strategies to support social and emotional development

Figure 4.3 This eight-year-old attends a mainstream primary school where she is supported by an inclusion support assistant for all of her learning. This enables her to access a highly personalised curriculum including participation in a nurture group.

Table 4.3 Teaching strategies to support social and emotional development

Supporting relationships	• Use social stories and scripts to explain to students how to behave in different social situations. Provide a script for each situation as children may not be able to generalise from one situation to another. Repetition of stories and scripts can help to embed them in CYP's memory, improving engagement, confidence, and understanding • Use puppets, role play, and drama to explore feelings and attitudes. This can help in improving peer relationships through language development and conversation • For paired activities, pair the child with an FASD with other children who are good role models, and plan groups carefully to ensure that the child with FASD has good role models to observe at all times • Plan for turn-taking games and circle games to encourage appropriate social interaction • For CYP who interrupt or find it hard to know when it is their turn, provide a concrete object such as a small ball as a holding item to indicate when it is appropriate to talk or have a go, i.e. when the ball is in the child's hand it is their turn • Provide the opportunity for supervised social situations with good role models in unstructured free time, including peer/buddy groups for break times and lunch times to facilitate friendships • Provide a key worker with whom the child can discuss social and emotional difficulties related to home or school life (this could be a teaching assistant, learning mentor or teacher) and who is well known to the child and with whom the child is able to bond (see Chapter 3 in relation to attachments) • Discuss with the child their general state of emotional well being at the beginning of each day using a scale from one to five, and record this in their planner. This can be used as a communication aid amongst support staff about the CYP's mood and ability to cope with the coming day. This may help to reduce anxiety throughout the day

Table 4.3 (continued)

Supporting relationships	• Discuss with the child, individually and in small group work, the many reasons why people bully others, including feelings of unhappiness, loneliness and frustration, illusions of power, and attempts to make themselves feel bigger and stronger. Use concrete examples and simple language
Supporting emotions	• Balance opportunities for the child to contribute and share ideas for group work and participate in group performances, then provide sufficient praise and encouragement to support them in these situations in order to build confidence
	• Use role play, social stories and scripts, and photographs to prepare the child for special events, including trips
	• Ensure parents/carers have advance notice of social events and trips so that they may prepare the child adequately
	• For trips make a book with photographs and pictures depicting what to expect during the trip. Include photos of the journey and what to expect on arrival. Share this with parents/carers
	• Some events (trips, concerts, etc.) may need to be discussed with parents first, in order that parents may decide whether it is appropriate for their child to be included. This will avoid any unnecessary disappointment for the child and assist with parental partnership
	• Carefully plan the child's transition to the chosen secondary school, further or higher education/work placement setting, ensuring liaison with parents/carers and other professionals involved in the child's support plan
	• Provide the child with a photographic record of their new school with members of staff, learning environments, new uniform, journey details and other important details included so that they can familiarise themselves with the new setting well before they arrive
Inappropriate interactions with others	• Provide low-impact one-to-one supervision where necessary and if possible a separate changing room for the student, such as an office. Ensure that the child is not left in a position where they are able to take advantage of other students, visitors, or members of staff. This will reduce the risk of the child acting on impulse and will make them more aware of how their behaviour impacts on others and enable them to improve peer relationships
	• Use role play and social scripts to talk through social scenarios and demonstrate appropriate and inappropriate interactions with others. Encourage appropriate understanding of 'self' through discussion time activities
	• Allow extra time for discussions to ensure understanding of basic information. A propensity for a child to expose themselves or touch others may simply be an attempt to engage others on an emotional level without understanding how others may feel or react
	• Sex education needs to highlight concrete rules that are easily understood and do not need to be generalised. For example, unprotected sex is *always* unsafe sex, condom use is *never* optional, and masturbation must *always* take place in private (ensuring an understanding of what private means). Consequences must be clearly and simply explained, using role play, social scripts, and repetition, and consistently applied
	• It may not be realistic to expect a child with an FASD to understand that unprotected sex may *or* may not end in pregnancy or disease, or that there is a time delay between intercourse, pregnancy, and the arrival of a baby. The delivery of these concepts may require careful planning, liaison with parents and carers, repetition and extra time for discussion and explanation
	• Engage external services to look for a community peer to support the child through social scenarios and provide positive role models
	• Consider inviting parents to sex education lessons so that discussions in the classroom can be extended at home using the same concepts and language in order to reduce any concerns parents may have about sex education
	• Monitor and record the incidence (including time of day, type of environment, particular room, other children involved, preceding incidents) of inappropriate interactions to determine any patterns and possible reasons, for example, stress or discomfort
	• Consider how the child can participate in external visits or community opportunities or take on prefect responsibilities within school and what kind of support they will need for this

Physical development

Many areas of physical development present challenges to CYP with FASDs. Their lack of understanding and inability to remember routines, interact appropriately with others, and make safe choices in everyday life impacts on their physical and emotional well being and general health. They can be easily led, which can result in substance abuse with inadequate understanding of the implications. In addition, medical conditions often experienced by children with FASDs, such as hearing and vision impairments, SPDs, and organ damage can result in poor sleep patterns, reduced dietary choices, and the need for medication.

The challenge for teachers is to be observant about when these children are lacking in energy levels because of lack of sufficient or appropriate food choices, or inadequate sleep or medical provision, and provide timely and effective intervention to support them in a sensitive manner in order that they can fully engage in learning.

Case study 4: physical development

David is 11 years old. He has strong literacy and speaking skills and enjoys drama. He has a positive and enthusiastic attitude to his learning. His challenges include difficulties with understanding abstract concepts, particularly money, and with seeing himself in an age-appropriate way. He demonstrates an eagerness to please, which could cause irritation amongst older peers, and he is working on his ability to manage conflict.

These challenges are combined with complex health needs, including visual and hearing impairments, heart problems (a leak in one of the valves), feeding problems, skeletal problems (his bones are not formed properly), mobility difficulties, which impact on his ability to walk distances and run, and double incontinence. There are also difficulties around feeding, food choices, small stature, and appropriate interactions with others, particularly unfamiliar adults.

David's health and dietary needs are met by a multi-disciplinary team who communicate effectively and regularly with parents, education staff, and the student in order to ensure that any lesson time missed through therapies and visits to the medical room is caught up to avoid student anxiety. He is encouraged to assess independently when he needs to visit the medical room for personal care needs.

David is encouraged to try very small amounts of new foods. Limiting what is on his plate and giving very clear targets for the amount he should try to eat helps to add variety to his diet. However, this needs to be balanced with the provision of opportunities for independence, as, although he can often eat more if he is fed by an adult, he is capable of feeding himself.

Strategies to support physical development

Figure 4.4 This 11-year-old attends a special school where his complex medical and health needs are supported alongside his learning needs by a range of professionals within the school.

Table 4.4 Teaching strategies to support physical development

Staff development	• Ensure understanding amongst all school staff of the range of difficulties the child may experience in relation to food and diet such as feeding and swallowing difficulties, reduced dietary choices/preferences, and health-related difficulties which may restrict diet and the amount of food the child can eat/digest
Lessons/ activities	• Provide opportunities for practical food technology lessons • Provide visual displays on food groups and healthy eating in the classroom and around the school • Encourage activity such as dancing outside of physical education lessons to improve activity and energy levels • Provide access to appropriate social experiences for leisure/eating activities during physical education and lunchtime • Provide opportunities for small group work planned around diet and healthy eating. This provides the opportunity for the child to ask questions that they may not be confident enough to ask in a large group situation
Snack/ lunchtime	• Set small achievable goals to encourage eating meals and trying new foods. Encourage the child to try one new food each week • Reduce the amount of food provided on a plate at any one time • Encourage the child to try small amounts of new foods and provide a clear target for the amount he/she should try to eat. Provide a variety of choices in meals • Share knowledge of the child's eating and dietary difficulties with all staff within the school
Medical issues	• Encourage medical staff, personal care staff, lunchtime staff, and teaching staff to work together on site to support the child to manage issues as unobtrusively as possible in order to build independence. This can result in improved relationships for the child with staff and peers

Table 4.4 (continued)

Medical issues	• Ensure thorough communication with parents about diagnosis/medical needs and cascade to all staff within school • Encourage speed in going to and returning from the medical room to minimise missed lesson time • Share news and inform the child what has been missed when they return to the classroom in order to reduce anxiety about missed lesson time
Personal hygiene issues	• Provide specific support around personal hygiene issues in individual and group work, including peer discussions relating to personal hygiene, as CYP with FASDs may need extrinsic motivation and frequent and constant reminders to remember hygiene routines

Being ready for employment

In order to prepare for their long-term future, CYP with FASDs need opportunities to engage in further education, employment, or training at the end of their compulsory education. They need to be ready for employment.

Children and young people with FASDs can experience difficulties in finding appropriate work experience placements, especially if they need one-to-one adult supervision for safeguarding and/or safety purposes. This will impact on their ability to find suitable employment opportunities. Further education and training opportunities will need to enhance the particular strengths that CYP with FASDs possess. These are usually in the area of practical skills.

Educators can help by ensuring that work placement providers, further and higher education establishments, and employers are properly informed about FASDs and how to support those affected. Preparation for employment and further education and training should include a focus on key life skills and understanding how and when to tell others that help and assistance is needed.

Case sudy 4: readiness for employment

Rob Wybrecht is a young man with an FASD. He works as a consultant offering expert support and advice to employers about including those affected by FASDs in the work place. He advises employers to remember that those with FASDs may have difficulties with the following:

- remembering a task with several parts;
- remembering verbal instructions;
- time management;
- staying focused;
- finishing one task before starting a new one;
- sleeping and waking up.

Rob offers the following tips to employers for success in supporting those affected by FASDs in the work place:

- Be willing to work with a job coach.
- Give concrete, concise instructions.
- Write instructions down and use pictures where possible.
- Demonstrate what you want done.
- It is often helpful for an employee with an FASD to work alongside a colleague.
- Create a laminated list with daily job duties for the employee to refer to.

Readiness for employment: preparing children and young people with fetal alcohol spectrum disorders for the future

Figure 4.5 This 19-year-old attends a special school where he is following the National Curriculum as well as a curriculum to support the development and acquisition of key life skills. He is looking forward to going to college to learn a practical skill such as mechanics or sport and leisure.

Table 4.5 Teaching strategies to support readiness for employment

Lessons/ activities	• Provide a personalised learning pathway which builds on the child's strengths and interests to facilitate employment opportunities and ensure that key life skills are in place • Provide plenty of concrete opportunities for handling money within mathematics, reinforced by community experiences of money handling such as visiting shops to buy specific items • Be prepared to spend additional curriculum time on work on self awareness and life skills through citizenship • Provide life skill experiences through PHSE, physical education, and social clubs and make time to listen to the student's concerns • Teach life skills specifically and frequently. Provide practical opportunities for shopping, cooking, car maintenance, cleaning, and other domestic chores • Encourage independence throughout school to develop individual personalities/talents. Allow students to use strategies to make their personal timetable more memorable (e.g. with the use of a highlighter); encourage them to organise their own snacks and water bottles for breaks, etc. • Facilitate discussions using social stories and scripts about employment, further and higher education, and career opportunities • Provide opportunities for the student to take on special roles within school where appropriate, such as prefect, class captain, or 'special helper', and provide support for those who might find this role difficult. Give the sudent small tasks to perform throughout the day such as taking the register to reception • Encourage the student to participate in enterprise activities such as fundraising for specific school goals, for example participating in the Christmas fair to raise money for a school trip or making items to be sold at fetes and fairs
Career choices	• Arrange visits to career fairs and exhibitions to demonstrate the range of work opportunities available • Arrange links with colleges of further education and higher education establishments to facilitate visits and information events • Ensure that the Careers Service and Connexions, together with parents/careers and voluntary organisations who support CYP with disabilities, are involved in the young person's transition plan • Provide opportunities for visits from appropriate professionals (e.g. 'People Who Help Us' for primary-aged children and career talks for secondary-aged students) • Provide opportunities for visits in the community, and work placement opportunities, ensuring that appropriate and informed adult support is in place to meet the CYP's needs

PHSE: Personal, Social, Health, and Economic Education.

Sustainability in the classroom

Children and young people with FASDs need an approach to teaching and learning which encompasses a number of key elements. This includes:

• a calm, uncluttered, structured learning environment;
• opportunities for small group work/small class sizes;
• small-step approaches to tasks, instructions, and activities;
• curricula/tasks which match their developmental and learning profile in all domains of development;
• opportunities to learn through visual and kinaesthetic mediums;
• frequent breaks from concentrated activities with opportunities for physical exercise;

- support with peer relationships, appropriate interaction with others, and learning key life skills.

By using these approaches, educators will support CYP with FASDs to consolidate and generalise their learning experiences in readiness for living experiences.

References

Birmingham City Council (2004) *Supporting Pupils with Autism Spectrum Disorder in Mainstream Secondary Schools*. DVD.

Blackburn, C. (2010) *Facing the Challenge and Shaping the Future for Primary and Secondary Aged Students with Foetal Alcohol Spectrum Disorders* (FAS-eD Project). London: National Organisation on Fetal Alcohol Syndrome (UK).

Brooks, T. (2010) 'Developing a learning environment which supports children with profound autistic spectrum disorders to engage as effective learners' (PhD thesis). Worcestershire: Institute of Education, Worcester University.

Carmichael Olson, H. and Gurgess, D.M. (1997) 'Early intervention for children prenatally exposed to alcohol and other drugs', in Guralnick, M.J (ed.) *The Effectiveness of Early Intervention*. Baltimore, MD: Paul H Brookes Publishing.

Carpenter, B. (2011) 'Pedagogically bereft! Improving learning outcomes for children with Foetal Alcohol Spectrum Disorders', *British Journal of Special Education*, 38 (1): 37–43.

Carpenter, B., Egerton, J., Brooks, T., Cockbill, B., Fotheringham, J., and Rawson, H. (2011) *The Complex Learning Difficulties and Disabilities Research Project: Developing Meaningful Pathways to Personalised Learning Final Report*. London: Specialist Schools and Academies Trust (SSAT).

Clarren, S.G.B. (2004) *Teaching Students with Fetal Alcohol Spectrum Disorder: Building Strengths, Creating Hope*. Edmonton, Canada: Alberta Learning.

DCSF (Department for Children Schools and Families) (2007) *The Children's Plan: Building Brighter Futures*. Edinburgh: The Stationery Office.

Kleinfeld, J. and Wescott, S. (eds) (1993) *Fantastic Antone Succeeds! Experiences in Educating Children with Fetal Alcohol Syndrome*. Fairbanks: University of Alaska Press.

Kleinfeld, J., Morse, B., and Wescott, S. (2000) *Fantastic Antone Grows Up*. Fairbanks: University of Alaska Press.

McPhillips, T., Bell, S., and Doveston, M. (2010) 'Overcoming barriers to the acquisition of literacy in twenty-first-century inclusive classrooms', in Rose, R. (ed.) *Confronting Obstacles to Inclusion: International Responses to Developing Inclusive Education*. Oxford: Routledge.

Streissguth, A.P. and Kanter, J. (eds) (1997) *The Challenges of Foetal Alcohol Syndrome: Overcoming Secondary Disabilities*. Seattle: University of Washington Press.

Wybrecht, R. (n.d.) *FASD Information for Employers: What Employers Need to Know about Individuals with FASD*. Boston.

Chapter 5

Fetal alcohol spectrum disorders and complex needs

Complex needs and children with fetal alcohol spectrum disorders

'Complex' is a word often used to describe children and young people (CYP) with fetal alcohol spectrum disorders (FASDs). What does it mean in the context of their learning? What are the implications for educating CYP with FASDs? What clues does it give us as we plan their individual education programme?

In the twenty-first century, CYP with complex learning difficulties and disabilities (CLDD) are presenting new profiles of learning needs, which we, as a teaching profession, have not yet resolved how to meet through our teaching style of curriculum or frameworks. We need to be honest about this – for the sake of our professional practice and, even more so, for the sake of the CYP. In relation to CYP with FASDs, educators can be described as 'pedagogically bereft' (Carpenter, 2011). This is not through professional negligence, but rather because, as society has changed in both its medical skill and moral code, a by-product has been a 'new breed' of children with complex disabilities, whose brain functioning is configured differently to that previously known to educators of children with disabilities (Goswami, 2008a).

The learning complexity of children and young people with fetal alcohol spectrum disorders

Children and young people with FASDs are certainly a unique group of learners, and their experiences formulate a unique and, at times, challenging perspective of this world. There are a number of elements that come together to create their often highly complex learning profile.

The breadth of learning difficulty

The term FASDs encompasses deficits in learning, attention, memory, and judgement. It also involves difficulties with receptive and expressive language, and in processing communication from others. Individuals with FASDs are often misdiagnosed because assessment outcomes focus on their behaviours, rather than the alcohol-caused brain damage (Streissguth *et al.*,

1996). Canadian research has shown that many CYP with FASDs are initially misdiagnosed with autistic spectrum disorder (ASD), Asperger syndrome (AS), attention deficit hyperactivity disorder (ADHD), and obsessive–compulsive disorder (OCD) (O'Malley, 2007).

Carr-Brown and Halle (2005) state that they believe 'that a proportion of children who have ADHD may have developed it as a result of the mother's drinking during pregnancy'. Their hypothesis is further extended by Kieran O'Malley (2007) (a psychiatrist with extensive experience of working with CYP with FASD), when he says, 'Children with FASD are true clinical masquerades and ADHD is their most likely disguise' (p. 185). Many UK school settings will not be aware that they have children with FASDs in their pupil population; they may be present, but with the alternative diagnoses described above.

The unevenness and inconsistency of the learning difficulties

The developmental profile of CYP with FASDs is variable, and this means that CYP with FASDs are difficult to accommodate within English National Curriculum Key Stages. Their expressive language may be in advance of their actual age, and their reading skills may be chronologically appropriate. However, in areas such as social skills and emotional maturity, they may be performing at half their developmental age. Mathematical and numerical concepts are particularly challenging for this group of children in that, for some, the parietal lobe, which controls numeracy and computational activity in the brain, may have significantly reduced functioning (Kopera-Frye et al., 1996; Goswami, 2004). However skilled an educator may be in differentiating the mathematics curriculum, if that part of the brain is not functioning effectively, just how do we teach mathematics to CYP with FASDs?

Figure 5.1, from the FASD Trust, powerfully illustrates just how unique the learning profile of CYP with FASDs can be.

Not only is the learning profile of CYP with FASDs uneven, or 'spiky', but their ability to carry out activities may vary from day to day. On one day they are able to accomplish a task, but on the next they cannot. This causes frustration to CYP and their educators. Educators often feel, mistakenly, that this inability is due to lack of self application on the part of the student, whereas it is a well-recognised feature of the learning profile of CYP with FASDs.

Secondary impact of difficulties

The prevalence of children with FASDs in foster care is five to ten times greater than the estimated prevalence (one to three per 1,000) in the general population (Astley et al., 2002; Astley, 2009). Children with FASDs come into care, on average, at a younger age than other children in care. As a result they spend a greater proportion of their lives in care and have a higher number of placements than their peers. This presents them with many additional life challenges, and they often remain involved in some form of welfare system into their adult lives (Burnside, 2009). As these CYP grow, they often experience poor mental health and disrupted

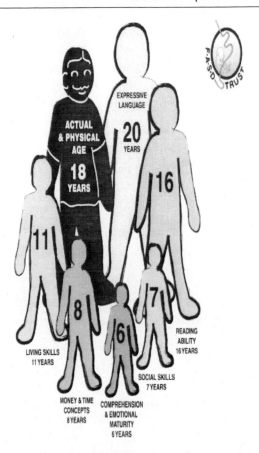

Figure 5.1 Developmental profile of an 18-year-old with an FASD. © FASD Trust/Jodee Kulp, www.betterendings.org.

school experience. It is reported that many CYP with FASDs will have early entry into the criminal justice system; Kelly (2009) reported that, above age 11 years, 60 per cent of CYPs with FASDs were in trouble with the law, and 50 per cent had experienced confinement. As adults, they may become homeless and chronically unemployed, and many do not complete compulsory education. Without intervention, they will become 'revolving door prisoners' (S. Meier, personal communication, 2008). Streissguth and colleagues (1996) found that 3 per cent of 6- to 11-year-olds, 12 per cent of 12- to 20-year-olds, and 23 per cent of adults from a cohort of 415 subjects diagnosed with FAS or fetal alcohol effects had attempted suicide. (The adult figure is five times the US national average.)

Compounding factors

It is clear that FASDs are multi-factorial (Autti-Ramo, 2002). In various studies, the women interviewed were not only consuming large amounts of alcohol, but also smoking and using drugs. Research shows that it is not only biomedical and psychological factors that give rise to complex needs, but also the interwoven experiences of poverty, educational disadvantage (Hirsch, 2007), and low educational achievement (Cassen and Kingdom, 2007). Social circumstances are also a factor – women living in poverty have been found to be more prone to binge drinking – and in some women genetic predisposition contributes to the impact of alcohol on the fetus (R. Gray, personal communication, November 2009).

Whatever the background of these CYP with FASDs, the challenge remains: how do we optimise learning for these CYP? Even more, we have to ask, how do we teach them? Often educators, being unaware of this group of CYP, do not identify them or plan specifically to meet their learning needs.

In the UK, recent research has begun to address this issue (see Blackburn, 2010) but much more needs to be done. Indeed, extensive practitioner-led, classroom-based research in Canada has led to the creation of specific curricula designed to address the unique learning needs of CYP with FASDs (Alton and Evenson, 2006).

Complex learning difficulties and disabilities and children and young people with fetal alcohol spectrum disorders

In this twenty-first-century society, complex learning difficulties and disabilities (CLDD) for CYP may be caused by some new medical or social phenomena, for example assisted conception or premature birth, maternal drug or alcohol abuse during pregnancy, or medical/genetic advances. CYP with FASDs form part of this wider group of CYP with CLDD. Their learning profile corresponds with the definition of CLDD established through the Complex Learning Difficulties and Disabilities Research Project supported by the Department for Education (Carpenter *et al.*, 2011) as described below.

Definition of complex learning difficulties and disabilities

Children and young people with CLDD have conditions that co-exist. These conditions overlap and interlock, creating a complex profile. The co-occurring and compounding nature of complex learning difficulties requires a personalised learning pathway that recognises CYP's unique and changing learning patterns. CYP with CLDD present with a range of issues and a combination of layered needs, including mental health, relationships, behavioural, physical, medical, sensory, communication and cognitive needs. They need informed specific support and strategies which may include transdisciplinary input to engage effectively in the learning process and to participate actively in classroom activities and the wider community. Their attainments may be inconsistent, presenting an atypical or uneven profile. In the school setting, learners may be working at any educational level, including the National Curriculum and P scales (Department for Education, 2012). This definition could also be applicable to learners in early years and post-school settings.

Conditions that coexist, overlap, and interlock

As described in the preceding chapters, there is an array of learning difficulties associated with FASDs: cognitive, behavioural/emotional, social, physical, and medical as well as learning difficulties. As well as a range of learning difficulties, CYP with FASDs may also have physical difficulties associated with the condition, including body organ and skeletal damage. For the young man described in the case study overview below (see pp. 73–76), FASD is made more complex through associated attachment disorder, behavioural, emotional, and social difficulties (BESD), and physical difficulties. There is a high correlation between young people with FASDs and mental health disorders, which can range from anxiety and stress to bipolar disorder, depression, and schizophrenia (Mukherjee *et al.*, 2006; Dubrovsky, 2009).

Requiring a personalised learning pathway

Educators need to respond to CYP with FASDs in a way that is respectful and affirmatory, and work with them where they are now. Personalised learning pathways need to build on the child's strengths and interests at an appropriate developmental level with realistic expectations from both child and educators. However, they need to incorporate strategies which take account of the child's difficulties with attention, distraction, and memory, and build bridges into learning for the student. Educational success for the student needs to be factored into any learning activity to allow them to achieve.

Transdisciplinary support

The key to educating CYP with FASDs successfully is a team approach involving representatives of all of the main agencies working with the child and their family. The most successful practice in this area adopts a transdisciplinary approach, whereby professionals transcend the disciplinary boundaries that often lock them into a particular style of single disciplinary practice. In working in the transdisciplinary style in the CLDD project, around the engagement of CYP with CLDD, including those with FASDs, Dr Michael Brown, Nurse Consultant for NHS Scotland (personal communication, 2010), observed:

> This transdisciplinary interactive approach to Engagement is evolving a common shared language and understanding that is applicable to all disciplines.

Combining professionals in a transdisciplinary team – around the child with an FASD – gives a powerful dynamic to the process of inquiry. Ultimately our goal for CYP with FASDs is to penetrate that mask of complexity which often shrouds their true learning needs, to then unlock their curiosity, release their motivation, and increase their participation.

An inconsistent, atypical, and uneven profile

By definition, all CYP with learning difficulties and disabilities have an uneven profile of learning. What distinguishes those with CLDD are the series of peaks and troughs in their overarching profile. It is what educators would call a 'spiky profile', represented for CYP with FASDs in Figure 5.1.

Working at any educational level

There are many CYP with FASD in mainstream schools. Again, Figure 5.1 illustrates that an 11-year-old with FASD could, in National Curriculum attainment terms, have literacy skills at level 5, but numeracy at P scale level 7. This is not uneven development; this is a spike!

Vulnerable children

Although these CYP with CLDD are not a homogenous group, their over-riding, unifying factor is 'vulnerability'. Figure 5.2 conceptualises the triggers for this vulnerability, which manifests in complex learning patterns, extreme behaviour patterns, and a range of socio-medical needs which are new and unfamiliar to many schools.

Children and young people with FASDs can fall anywhere on the continuum of vulnerability because of disadvantage, economic or social deprivation, or disability. Although education may not be able to overturn poverty in our society, it can build resilient CYP:

> Resilience factors are those processes which buffer or minimise the effects of adverse stimuli on a person.

> (Carpenter, 2012)

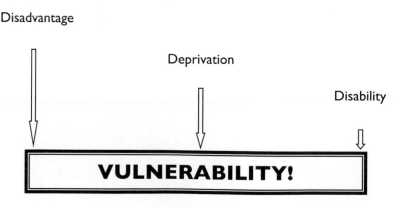

Figure 5.2 The continuum of vulnerability.

Research and practice have shown (Pretis and Dimova, 2008) that, where CYP experienced educational successes, their self esteem was raised, enabling them to develop a level of emotional resilience which, in turn, raised their opportunities in life. This is at the heart of educational transformation: the capacity to transform a child's life for the better. Never was this aspiration more applicable than in the education we offer CYP with FASDs.

New generation pedagogy

To educate these twenty-first-century CYP meaningfully, effectively, and purposefully we must evolve new generation pedagogy. This pedagogy needs to be within the framework of practice that currently exists in schools. Our layers of pedagogy in the classroom therefore become 'for all'; 'additional'; 'new, innovative, and personalised'. The components of new generation pedagogy are described below.

Curriculum calibration

The often variable profile of need and attainment of CYP with CLDD scan easily result in a fragmented curriculum which lacks cohesion, congruence, and continuity. In curriculum calibration, CYP's profile of need is critically reviewed, and their patterns of engagement profiled. A personalised curriculum experience is sought to match each strand of their learning needs.

Pedagogical reconciliation

This may require 'pedagogical re-engineering': adapting or adjusting an approach from our existing teaching repertoire. In this process, we carefully analyse the structure and components of other successful pedagogies in the field of special educational needs (Lewis and Norwich, 2005), and match them to a new generation of CYP with CLDD. This is a process of analysis, deduction, and refinement, reconciling those pedagogies to CYP's unique profile of learning.

Creation of new and innovative teaching strategies

Alongside pedagogical reconciliation is the need to create and innovate a new pedagogy that is responsive to the new profile of learning needs presented by this evolving cohort of CYP with CLDD. What are the teaching strategies that will enable us to engage these CYP as active participants in the dynamics of our lessons, programmes, or learning environments? We need specific interventions (Wolke, 2009).

Personalising learning pathways

Personalising learning enables us to mould the learning experience directly around CYP with CLDD. To do this we have to discover the learning needs and pathways of these very diverse CYP, and establish their learning capacity and learning effectiveness. CYP with CLDD have to see relevance and to find themselves truly engaged in a dynamic and coherent process of learning that makes sense to them.

Finding ways to teach children with fetal alcohol spectrum disorders

There is a great educational vulnerability around CYP with FASDs, which means that the current style and structure of many classrooms is not conducive to engaging them as effective learners. Many of their behavioural traits militate against sustained learning with cumulative gains. As one mother, Julia Brown, the founder of the FASD Trust, stated:

> It's like living with someone who is drunk. They are clumsy, suffer memory loss, and display socially inappropriate behaviour. They think they are invincible: that they are Superman and can fly!

In terms of classroom practice, there are profound implications for teaching CYP with FASDs. As Porter and Ashdown (2002, p. 16) point out with reference to complex needs:

> This is a wide and varied group of learners. They include pupils who do not simply require a differentiated curriculum or teaching at a slower pace, but who, at times, require further adaptations to teaching if they are to make progress.

This seriously challenges our pedagogy and how we teach. What is more than differentiation, if differentiation is the process of adjusting teaching to meet individual needs?

Challenges and responses

Educators will ask 'what will these defining characteristics look like as "learning" in my classroom?' Based on recent research in UK classrooms (Blackburn, 2010; Carpenter, 2011), the following is a summary of some of the key 'learning challenges' for CYP with FASD:

1 slower processing pace;
2 memory problems;
3 gaps and inconsistencies in understanding;
4 difficulty in processing and sequencing auditory information;

5   impulsivity and distractibility;
6   anxiety about change;
7   incomplete concept of self;
8   social interaction and peer group difficulties;
9   limited attention span;
10 hyperactivity and inattentiveness.

This is where we have to meet the complex needs of CYP with FASDs, with fresh, creative pedagogy: 'We must seek to build an inclusive curriculum . . . around adaptation, modification and design . . . that will be relevant to all learners' (Carpenter *et al.*, 2002).

Finding ways to teach children and young people with fetal alcohol spectrum disorders

Engaging children and young people with fetal alcohol spectrum disorders

A key output from the Specialist Schools and Academies Trust (SSAT) Complex Needs Project (http://complexld.ssatrust.org.uk) has been that the new pedagogy required for this group of learners, including those with FASDs, needs to be built on 'engagement' (Figure 5.3):

> Sustainable learning can occur only when there is meaningful engagement. The process of engagement is a journey which connects a child and their environment (including people, ideas, materials and concepts) to enable learning and achievement.
>
> (Carpenter *et al.*, 2011)

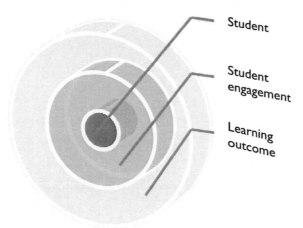

Figure 5.3 Relationship between engagement and learning.

Literature has widely endorsed that 'for CYP with disabilities . . . engaged behaviour is the single best predictor of successful learning' (Iovannone *et al.*, 2003, in Brooks, 2010, p. 86). It is the bridge between CYP and their learning target. Engagement not only enhances the process of differentiation; it personalises it, leading to what can be termed 'personalised engagement'. This concept builds on, and refines for this group of CYP, the process of personalising learning advocated by David Hargreaves (2006, p. 6):

> Personalising learning demands that schools transform their response to the learner from the largely standardised to the profoundly personalised . . . If students are to engage in deeper learning, they will need new forms of enriched support.

Engagement is a powerful vehicle for the CYP voice as the child, either through voice or by implication, demonstrates their preferences for engagement style and the pathway by which, and through which, they will engage.

The complex learning difficulties and disabilities engagement for learning approach

The Engagement Profile and Scale is a classroom tool developed through SSAT's research into effective teaching and learning for CYP with CLDD. It allows educators to focus on CYP's engagement as learners and create personalised learning pathways. It prompts CYP-centred reflection on how to increase the learners' engagement, leading to deep learning. Engagement is multi-dimensional, and encompasses awareness, curiosity, investigation, discovery, anticipation, persistence, and initiation. By focusing on these seven indicators of engagement within the Engagement Profile and Scale, teachers can ask themselves questions such as: 'How can I change the learning activity to stimulate Robert's curiosity?' or 'What can I change about this experience to encourage Shannon to persist?' The adaptations made and the effect on CYP's level of engagement can be monitored and recorded, together with a score on the engagement scale. Over time, it is possible to chart the success of interventions and adjustments, and the effect this has had on the child's levels of engagement. This can then be applied to other learning situations for the child.

Schools and individual educators may already focus on engagement for their CYP, but often this valuable and time-consuming personalising of learning goes unrecorded and the outcomes unmonitored. The Engagement Profile and Scale offers a means of doing both.

Using the complex learning difficulties and disabilities project's Engagement Profile and Scale

Classroom accommodation, adaptation, and amelioration are required to engage CYP with FASDs as effective learners. The following is a case study of a young man with an FASD who was involved in the CLDD Research Project. It describes an intervention devised by his class team, and structured and monitored using the Engagement Profile and Scale. The intervention resulted in his increased engagement and independence in learning, and was able to be generalised to other lessons.

Introduction

Naseem (not his real name) is a young man of 15 years who has been diagnosed with an FASD and moderate learning difficulties, made more complex by attachment disorder and BESD. He also has growth issues and talipes bilateral. His teacher had reviewed Naseem's learning, and concluded that one of his most important barriers to learning was his apparent inability to complete tasks and activities. This target was therefore established as a priority learning need for Naseem, and became the focus for the intervention.

Using the Engagement Profile and Scale

The Engagement Profile and Scale works on the principle of enabling a student's engagement through personalisation of an activity or learning task which enables that individual to attain their learning targets. It offers a way of recording the pathways and monitoring outcomes of personalising learning through an engagement score.

Completing the Engagement Profile

An Engagement Profile was drawn up for Naseem by observing him taking part in a favourite activity and describing his actions against each of the seven engagement indicators. This allowed all educators to recognise the level of engagement that Naseem was capable of and the kind of behaviours they were aiming for in other activities. It helped them to develop high expectations for Naseem.

Establishing a priority learning need

His teacher and teaching assistants identified his individual strengths, difficulties, and motivators so that the activity could be personalised to increase his engagement with it. His difficulties, in common with many students with FASDs, were a high level of distractibility and the need for continual reminders and prompts from the staff working with him to keep him on task.

Naseem's first target was to complete his class job of setting the table for snack time. Keeping in mind Naseem's barriers, the teacher used the following strategies – introduced over a number of sessions – to allow Naseem to achieve success:

1   She developed a series of visual photographic prompts for each part of Naseem's task to aid his memory retention. The photographs were initially sequenced in the right order as he found sequencing difficult, but in later sessions, to extend Naseem's independence, he was given responsibility for sequencing the photos.

2   The teacher physically modelled and rehearsed with Naseem how to use the photographs to build on his kinaesthetic learning strengths, rather than relying on auditory instruction, which Naseem struggled to process and retain.

3   Students with FASDs need repetition of facts or requests many times, as they have difficulties with retaining learning. Use of the visual prompts allowed a continuing permanent reminder to Naseem of the task he was doing and the steps he needed to make to complete it. It is important to 'script' the task or activity so that the student can link fragments of knowledge and make a 'whole' response.

4   The teacher praised Naseem, increasing his self esteem and self confidence. It is also important to share a student's achievement with their family, so that they can further reinforce the success.

In this way, the teacher supported Naseem to keep active as a learner and to experience success.

Monitoring outcomes using the Engagement Scale

Naseem's baseline engagement was documented using the Engagement Scale before the intervention took place. This allowed the teacher to show Naseem's progress from his original level of engagement with the activity, before the intervention, to his post-intervention level, after the intervention was in place.

Figure 5.4 shows the intervention engagement outcomes for Naseem over a two-month period. The 'pre' marker shows Naseem's level of engagement before his teacher put the interventions in place. The 'post 1' line shows Naseem's progress in completing his classroom job. As Naseem increased in his ability to engage with the activity, the teacher added new elements to extend and expand his learning. These extensions broadly correspond to dips in his engagement as each unfamiliar element was included within his photographic task instructions, and then increasing engagement as his confidence grew. The extensions to the task were introduced as shown in Table 5.1.

Following Naseemj's success using the sequenced photo cues for completing his class task, the teacher decided to generalise this strategy to his science lessons. Previously, Naseem had never been able to set up the equipment for his science experiments, so it was hoped that the photo cues strategy would be effective in this situation. His teacher created a set of photos showing each piece of science equipment needed for a practical and where in the classroom they were to be found, with a final photo of how the equipment should look when it was set up.

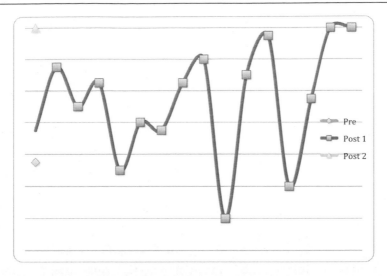

Figure 5.4 Graph showing Naseem's engagement for learning outcomes monitored using the Engagement Profile and Scale (x-axis: session number over a two-month period; y-axis: Engagement Scale score).

Table 5.1 Strategies for completing a personalised target

Target 1:To complete allocated class job (see Figure 5.4: Post 1)
Strategy 1:Visual schedule – eight photographs in correct order to support completion of activity (session 1)
Strategy 2: Eight photographs in incorrect order to support independence in completion of activity (sessions 2–6)
Strategy 3: Peers instructed not to interact with Naseem (session 6)
Strategy 4:Additional job: to make drinks to give him more responsibility (session 7)
Strategy 5: Fewer photos (five) (session 8)
Strategy 6:Additional job: putting cups out (session 9)
Strategy 7: One additional photo introduced for additional element of task (sessions 10 and11)
Strategy 8:Additional job: to pour drinks (sessions 12–16)

Naseem entered the science room, set out his photos, and collected the equipment. He got only one piece wrong, bringing a glass rod rather than a thermometer, but he was able to correct this when questioned what the photo was. He then set up the equipment perfectly apart from putting the thermometer in upside down.

The 'post 2' marker in Figure 5.4 shows the success of this intervention. His teacher noted in the Engagement Scale comment boxes:

> Naseem went straight to where his photos are kept, put them out in correct order and looked at them . . . He started the task without being needed to be told . . . It was a massive improvement; he completed the whole task without the teacher needing to intervene and keep him on task.

The teacher concluded of the intervention: 'It was an amazing success. I will now start to photograph all practicals to have a set of photo packages for all CYP to use.'

This case study overview shows the benefits for both CYP and educators of personalising learning for CYP using appropriate strategies (concrete visual cues, modelling, and praise) to meet the acknowledged learning strengths (visual/kinaesthetic learning style) and needs (distractibility and difficulties with memory) of CYP with FASDs, based on the concept of engagement in learning.

Conclusion

Engagement is the bridge between CYP and their learning target. Without engagement there is no deep learning (Hargreaves, 2006), effective teaching, meaningful outcome, real attainment, or quality progress (Carpenter, 2010). CYP with CLDD need to be taught in ways that match their individual learning styles by educators who recognise their abilities and potential for engagement in learning. Our work must be to transform CYP with CLDD into active learners by releasing their motivation, unlocking their curiosity, and increasing their participation. A focus on engagement can underpin a process of personalised inquiry through which the teacher can develop effective learning experiences. Using evidence-based knowledge of a child's successful learning pathways, strategies can be identified, high expectations set, and incremental progress recorded on their journey towards optimal engagement in learning.

These 'partnerships in learning' are vital if we are to unravel the complexity of the learning profile for CYP with CLDD, for, as Rose (2010, p. 13) says:

> If we are to move beyond the tokenistic we have to develop a commitment to engagement based upon mutual respect rather than seeing one part of such partnerships simply as a source of information.

Through this process of creating a personalised pathway to learning, educators find themselves involved in intricate inquiry: exploring, investigating, and discovering.

This was observed many times during the CLDD Research Project, with one headteacher noting:

> You have to acknowledge that you don't have all the answers. Contexts and children have changed dramatically. We need a 'finding out culture' in schools.

To achieve this, we must find ways of implementing structured opportunities for the professional development of school staff to ensure that new professional capacities are supported. We have to acquire new professional skills, and more creative and responsive styles of teaching, if we are to meet the challenge of engagement for CYP with FASDs specifically and CLDD more widely.

Looking to the future, there is a strong argument for strengthening the interface between neuroscience and education. Information from neuroscience (Sousa, 2007) could significantly influence how we develop future pedagogy for CYP with FASDs. Access to the anatomy and physiology of the developing brain will further contribute to the accuracy of diagnosis, and enable us to better understand how CYP with FASDs learn (Giedd and Rapoport, 2010). It could raise the attainment of these vulnerable children as our teaching becomes better matched to their learning styles. Goswami (2008b, p. 16) writes:

> Scientific advances in genetics and neuroimaging offer a potential opportunity within the next 20 years to identify children with learning difficulties in infancy . . . Such advances will eventually enable environmental interventions from infancy which would alter developmental learning trajectories for these children with consequent benefits throughout the life course.

For and with CYP with FASDs, we must navigate their routes to learning. Armed with the tools of personalisation (Hargreaves, 2005), we must innovate a responsive pedagogy, one that will transform the life chances of these CYP. If we do not, many CYP with FASDs will be lost in, and to, our school system: cognitively disenfranchised, socially dysfunctional, and emotionally disengaged. As educators we must acquire the knowledge, understanding, and skills to equip them to enjoy active citizenship in twenty-first-century society.

References

Astley, S.J. (2009) 'Prevalence of FAS in foster care', in Jonsson, E., Dennett, L., and Littlejohn, G. (eds) *Fetal Alcohol Spectrum Disorder (FASD): Across the Lifespan*. Edmonton, Canada: Institute of Health Economics.

Astley, S.J., Stachowiak, J., Clarren, S.K., and Clausen, C. (2002) 'Application of the fetal alcohol syndrome facial photographic screening tool in a foster care population', *Journal of Pediatrics*, 141 (5): 712–717.

Autti-Ramo, I. (2002) 'Foetal alcohol syndrome: a multifaceted condition', *Developmental Medicine & Child Neurology*, 44: 141–144.

Blackburn, C. (2010) *Facing the Challenge and Shaping the Future for Primary and Secondary Aged Students with Foetal Alcohol Spectrum Disorders* (FAS-eD Project). London: National Organisation on Fetal Alcohol Syndrome (UK). Online at: www.nofas-uk.org/news.htm#tdanews, accessed 16 September 2011.

Brooks, T. (2010) 'Developing a learning environment which supports children with profound Autistic Spectrum Disorder to engage as effective learners' (PhD thesis). Coventry: Coventry University/ University of Worcester.

Burnside, L. (2009) 'Impact on system usage within foster care', in Jonsson, E., Dennett, L., and Littlejohn, G. (eds) *Fetal Alcohol Spectrum Disorder (FASD): Across the Lifespan*. Edmonton, Canada: Institute of Health Economics.

Carpenter, B. (2010) *A Vision for 21st Century Special Education*. London: Specialist Schools and Academies Trust.

Carpenter, B. (2011) 'Pedagogically bereft! Improving learning outcomes for children with foetal alcohol spectrum disorders', *British Journal of Special Education*, 38 (1): 37–43.

Carpenter, B. (2012) 'Building emotional resilience and building positive mental health'. Keynote address to the International Conference on Global Students Global Schools, Abu Dhabi, United Arab Emirates (22 February).

Carpenter, B., Ashdown, R., and Bovair, K. (2002) *Enabling Access: Effective Teaching and Learning for Children with Learning Difficulties* (2nd edn). London: David Fulton.

Carpenter, B., Egerton, J., Brooks, T., Cockbill, B., Fotheringham, J., and Rawson, H. (2011) *The Complex Learning Difficulties and Disabilities Research Project: Developing Meaningful Pathways to Personalised Learning Final Report*. London: Specialist Schools and Academies Trust. Online at: http://complexld.ssatrust.org.uk/, accessed 24 February 2012.

Carr-Brown, J. and Halle, M. (2005) 'Twitches that indicate alcohol may hurt babies', *Sunday Times*, 20 November 2005.

Cassen, R., and Kingdom, G. (2007) *Tackling Low Educational Achievement*. London: Joseph Rowntree Foundation. Online at: www.jrf.org.uk/sites/files/jrf/2063-education-schools-achievement.pdf, accessed 16 September 2011.

Department for Education (2012) 'About performance scales (P scales)'. London: DfE. Online at: http://www.education.gov.uk/schools/teachingandlearning/assessment/a00203453/about-performance-scales-p-scales, accessed 28 February 2012.

Dubrovsky, D. (2009) 'Co-morbidities with mental health for an individual with FASD', in Jonsson, E., Dennett, L., and Littlejohn, G. (eds) *Fetal Alcohol Spectrum Disorder (FASD): Across the Lifespan*. Edmonton: Institute of Health Economics.

Giedd, J.N. and Rapoport, J.L. (2010) 'Structural MRI of paediatric brain development: what have we learned and where are we going?', *Neuron*, 67 (5): 728–734.

Goswami, U. (2004) 'Neuroscience, education and special education', *British Journal of Special Education*, 31 (4): 175–183.

Goswami, U. (2008a) *Cognitive Development: The Learning Brain*. East Sussex: Psychology Press.

Goswami, U. (2008b) *Learning Difficulties: Future Challenges* (Foresight Mental Capital and Well Being Project). London: Government Office for Science.

Hargreaves, D. (2006) *A New Shape for Schooling?* London: Specialist Schools and Academies Trust.

Hirsch, D. (2007) *Experiences of Poverty and Educational Disadvantage*. London: Joseph Rowntree Foundation. Online at: www.actiononaccess.org/download.php?f=1347, accessed 24 August 2009.

Iovannone, R., Dunlap, G., Huber, H., and Kincaid, D. (2003) 'Effective educational practices for students with autism spectrum disorders', *Focus on Autism and Other Developmental Disabilities*, 18: 150–166.

Kopera-Frye, K., Dehaene, S., and Streissguth, A.P. (1996) 'Impairments in number-processing induced by prenatal alcohol exposure', *Neuropsychologia*, 34: 1187–1196.

Kelly, K. (2009) 'Is Foetal Alcohol Spectrum Disorder linked to anti-social behaviour?', *Woman's Hour*, Radio 4. Online at: www.bbc.co.uk/radio4/womanshour/03/2009_16_mon.shtml, accessed 20 April 2009.

Lewis, A. and Norwich, B. (eds) (2005) *Special Teaching for Special Children: Pedagogies for Inclusion*. Milton Keynes: Open University Press.

Mukherjee, R.A.S., Hollins, S., and Turk, J. (2006) 'Psychiatric comorbidity in foetal alcohol syndrome', *Psychiatric Bulletin*, 30: 194–195.

O'Malley, K.D. (ed.) (2007) *ADHD and Fetal Alcohol Spectrum Disorders*. New York: Nova Science Publishers.

Porter, J. and Ashdown, R. (2002) *Pupils with Complex Needs: Promoting Learning through Visual Methods and Materials*. Tamworth: NASEN.

Pretis, M. and Dimova, A. (2008) 'Vulnerable children of mentally ill parents: towards evidence-based support for improving resilience', *Support for Learning*, 23 (3): 152–160.

Rose, R. (2010) 'The involvement of young people with learning disabilities in an international conference: moving beyond the factual to challenge our ides on inclusion', *PMLD Link*, 22 (1): 11–15.

Sousa, D.A. (2007) *How the Special Needs Brain Learns*. Thousand Oaks, CA: Corwin Press.

Streissguth, A., Barr, H., Kogan, J., and Bookstein, F. (1996) *Understanding the Occurrence of Secondary Disabilities in Clients with Fetal Alcohol Syndrome (FAS) and Fetal Alcohol Effects (FAE)*. Final Report. Centers for Disease Control and Prevention Grant No. 04/CCR008515. Seattle, WA: University of Washington Fetal Alcohol and Drug Unit.

Wolke, D. (2009) 'Long term outcomes of extremely pre-term children: implications for early childhood intervention'. Paper to the Early Intervention Conference, Madrid, Spain (November).

Chapter 6

Family dynamics

The support needs and experiences of the families of children with fetal alcohol spectrum disorders

Parents and carers are children and young people's (CYP) first and most enduring educators and their role in their children's educational journey should be valued. For the parents of a child with a special educational need or disability, this message is critical for educators to understand. In this situation, the child's journey in the years before they arrive at school can often be complex and families may have experienced a range of conflicting and difficult emotions in travelling this journey with their child.

When informed that their child has a disability, whether it is at birth or at a later date, families can experience a range of emotions and feelings. Often professionals assume that families will be devastated by the news of their child's disability, but it is important to remember that some families will not (Carpenter and Egerton, 2006). Jill Davies (2005), carrying out interviews with families as part of the First Impressions project (Foundation for People with Learning Disabilities [FPLD], 2005) was told by a mother who was delighted with the birth of her baby (who had Down syndrome): 'If someone had offered their commiserations I would have been very upset' (p. 5). Davies noted, quoting Kearney and Griffin (2001; Davies, 2005), that some professionals find it difficult to accept such a stance, assuming that parents who do not show distress after the diagnosis are in a state of denial:

> Every time I expressed my joy to the staff at the hospital, they said, 'She's denying reality.' I understood the reality of my child's situation but, for me, there was another reality.
>
> (Kearney and Griffin, 2001, p. 583)

Some families may experience mixed emotions. The impact of having a child with complex physical health needs in the family has a combination of positive and negative consequences: a combination of joy (at achievements however limited) and sorrow (from missed opportunities and distress experienced). Many parents and siblings demonstrate tremendous resilience and develop a range of effective coping strategies that help them to respond to the challenges they encounter (McConkey, 2007).

For other families, the experience can result in a range of emotions that require support from friends, extended family, and professionals. These include fear, isolation, anxiety, loneliness, guilt, anger, worry for the future, shock, terror, intense fatigue, jealousy, grief, depression (requiring medication and time off work), impotency, protectiveness, defensiveness, despondency, frequent panic attacks, and sometimes relief that they finally have a diagnosis after months of battling with health professionals to be referred for assessment (Carpenter, 2005; Blackburn, 2008). These feelings may be even more complex when children are born with a disability that is preventable and/or the family structure is unusual, such as those affected by prenatal alcohol or drug exposure.

Children and young people affected by prenatal alcohol exposure often come to the attention of protective service agencies; they frequently enter foster care and may be placed for adoption (Astley et al., 2002; May et al., 2006). A study of CYP in foster care in Washington, USA, found that among the sample of CYP who were fostered, the prevalence of fetal alcohol syndrome (FAS) was 10 to 15 times greater than in the general population. Streissguth and colleagues (1985) identified that 73 to 80 per cent of CYP with full-blown FAS are in foster or adoptive placement. CYP may experience a number of foster placements (up to 16 placements for one young person aged 16 has been reported; O'Malley, personal communication, 2010) before they are placed in an adoptive family. For CYP with fetal alcohol spectrum disorders (FASDs), therefore, the family structure may consist of foster or adoptive parents and family members as well as, or instead of, their biological family. Therefore sensitivity about relationship difficulties and family dynamics is required, particularly in relation to any attachment difficulties the CYP may be experiencing as a result of early life experiences.

Attachment

Attachment theory was first formulated by Bowlby (1969) as a way of explaining the observed responses of young children and infants to separation from a primary adult. CYP will develop a particular pattern of attachment to this primary adult (usually the mother) according to the adult's response to the infant's early overt and subtle communication signals (cries, responses to face-to-face interactions and language). Building on this, Ainsworth and colleagues (1978) and Main and Solomon (1986) identified different patterns/styles of attachment, including:

- secure attachment pattern;
- insecure attachment pattern, including
  - organised attachment patterns;
    - avoidant pattern;
    - resistant/ambivalent pattern;
  - disorganised attachment pattern.

These attachment patterns/styles are first evident between 9 and 12 months (Specialist Schools and Academies Trust, 2010). In order to have a secure base from which to explore the world, be resilient to stress, and have meaningful relationships with themselves and others, all infants need a primary adult who cares for them sensitively and who perceives, makes sense of, and responds to their needs (Sergeant, 2010, pp. 35–36).

Effective primary adults will respond to the cues of the infant in a way that is appropriate to that individual child. The infant is learning about him/herself by being understood by another; this is also the basis of the infant subsequently learning about others and about empathy for others. The outcome of warm satisfying experiences of early relationships is that CYP are more likely to have a positive sense of self, to make close and lasting relationships with others (Main and Cassidy, 1988), and to develop a *secure attachment pattern/style*.

However, a parent/carer's ability to meet their infant's needs sensitively can be disrupted by a number of factors, including:

- illness (mother and/or child), including postnatal depression;
- the birth of a child with a disability for whom parents are unprepared emotionally;
- maternal drug/alcohol or other substance abuse;
- frequent moves and placements in the case of a child who is fostered/adopted from birth (including multiple foster placements/adoptions);
- removal of the child from the home environment for safeguarding or other purposes;
- lack of response from the infant to the mother's care;
- traumatic experiences.

This can result in the unavailability or unpredictability of a primary adult to meet an infant's needs, causing the infant to adopt an *insecure attachment pattern/style* (see above). This can have an impact on the way in which he/she forms later relationships and can be particularly problematic if he/she moves into new homes (for fostering and adoption placements). CYP with FASDs may be exposed to one or more of these factors in their early years and can be particularly vulnerable to attachment difficulties as a result.

Children and young people with attachment difficulties (insecure attachment patterns) can be difficult to parent and will require patience and understanding. Families will need to be equipped with knowledge about attachment difficulties and the impact they have on children's development, education, and behaviour. Educators can support parents by signposting them to relevant agencies who may be able to support them in understanding the nature of their child's difficulties (see Chapter 1).

In addition, CYP with insecure attachment patterns will need extra support in the classroom. In particular, they will need access to educators who can respond sensitively and predictability to their behaviour and learning needs and who understand the implications of attachment pattern/style on their relationships with others as well as their relationships with classroom tasks (see Chapter 3 on how FASDs impact on learning).

Cultural aspects of attachment

The cultural aspects of infant–caregiver relationships and early attachment development are too wide for a broad discussion within this publication. However, it is important to note that understanding attachment patterns/styles must be located within cultural values and dynamics in order for all CYP, from a range of cultures and backgrounds, to be understood in this context.

The literature points to evidence that the survival (and development) of infants depends on bonds with caregivers who protect and nurture them. The psychological literature in particular presents caregiver–child relationships in terms of an innate bond of attachment between an infant and primary caregiver (usually the mother) (Rogoff, 2003). However, the nature of infant relationships and attachments differs across cultures and the European American middle-class mother–child relations upon which much attachment research has been based may not transfer easily to other cultures. In cultures, for example, where there remains a high birth rate and infant mortality rate (such as in shanty towns in Brazil), parents' attention will be devoted to survival of the infant past the infancy stage, before thoughts and attention can turn to emotional attachment with any individual child (ibid.). As Scheper-Hughes (1985) notes:

> Theories of innate maternal scripts such as 'bonding', 'maternal thinking' or 'maternal instincts' are both culture and history bound, the reflection of a very specific and recent reproductive strategy: to give birth to a few babies and to invest heavily in each one.
>
> (cited in Rogoff, 2003, p. 113)

Thus, although most European American infants can be observed in the Strange Situation experiment (Ainsworth *et al.*, 1978)[1] to fit the secure attachment pattern, the anxious/avoidant pattern is more common in studies in western European countries and the anxious/resistant pattern is more common in studies located in Israel and Japan (Rogoff, 2003). This would seem to fit cultural values and practices where early independence training (Germany) may be a common approach to early caregiving (ibid.), or where infants are unfamiliar with being left with strangers (Japan) (Miyake *et al.*,1985). Rogoff (2003, p. 116) notes that infants' attachments are intimately related to community arrangements of childcare, reflecting historical circumstances and cultural values regarding families' roles in caregiving. Childcare may involve extended family, other community/village adults, nurses in communal nurseries, older siblings, or CYP within the same community. A range of attachment patterns/styles will be observed in CYP with FASDs that will reflect the cultural environment(s) to which they have been exposed in their early childhood.

Birth families

If a child with an FASD is living with their biological family, sensitivity and understanding about how parents may be feeling about the cause of their child's disability is paramount. For the birth parents of a child with an FASD, the experience of feeling guilt can be overwhelming and impact significantly on the relationship between mother and CYP. A birth mother (Whitehurst, 2010) describes this profound experience:

> I think all the time I was trying to find out if this was what was wrong. I was able to put a lot of my personal stuff aside because I was fighting so hard for him, but when you actually get that diagnosis it's like, 'Oh my, oh boy, what have I done?'. . . It's very hard to forgive yourself when you've actually damaged someone's life irrevocably, you know. You can't turn the clock back . . . I've said sorry to him so many times, and said I really, really wouldn't have wanted this life for you, and I really am so sorry . . . but all I can do is be there for you to help you get through it, you know.
>
> (p. 43)

Educators can support birth parents by offering a non-judgemental, empathetic listening ear, and by recognising that the birth parent of a child with FASD will undoubtedly have experienced a degree of grief about their child's condition, and will be 'living with the burden of the legacy this has left' (ibid., p. 52). As one mother stated, when asked what kind of support the family needed in raising their son (with FASD):

> The thing we need most is help to deal with the guilt and gel as a family.
> (Anonymous parent, personal communication, 2010)

Adoptive families

A discussion of the adoption process is important to highlight the need for understanding about the emotional trauma this process may have inflicted on adoptive parents (and CYP), in order that educators may be empathetic towards families' concerns about their child.

> Adoption begins with a process to parent a child not born or conceived of one's own body. Adoptive families are thus intentional families bound together by belief, will, practice and most of all love.
> (Rampage et al., 2003, p. 210)

The decision to adopt a child is not one that any adult will enter into lightly and can result from a number of factors, including (Rampage et al., 2003, p. 212):

- Infertility or the inability to carry a pregnancy to full term
- The desire to provide a stable home environment for a relative (e.g. niece or nephew) when the child's parents are unavailable due to long term illness (including drug or alcohol addiction or mental illness) or death
- The desire to extend a family without the necessity for pregnancy

- A religious or social desire to provide care for someone less fortunate
- The desire for a single person or gay/lesbian couple to parent a child.

The process of adoption can be necessarily lengthy, complex, and intrusive in order to ensure that suitable and appropriate home environments are provided for vulnerable CYP.

The challenges faced by all families in daily life are also faced by adoptive families. In addition to this, adoptive families face the additional challenge that every adopted child will have two families (the family with whom the child lives and the family they have left behind). The child may have memories about their birth parents and strong feelings of attachment towards them, impacting on the success of the adoptive placement and their relationship with adoptive parents and other adults (see earlier section on attachment). Although very happy in her adopted family, one teenager outlines her interest in her birth family:

> I just wanted to say that sometimes I often wonder what it would have been like if I lived with my birth mum, if she didn't drink and I still lived with her and my brother and sister – what life would have been like. I just wonder, and then I say to myself, 'Well, I don't live with her, and I never have, and I never will, so I just have to get on with life,' and then I do.
> (Girl with an FASD, aged 13, personal communication, 2010)

This video highlights another family's experience of adoption: http://www.youtube.com/watch?v=oj95GyEMZ_4.

Ethical issues of adoption

Families may need support from educators as they struggle with the realities of adoption. They may not have received full information at the time of the adoption or may not have foreseen the impact it would have on their family. In highlighting ethical issues surrounding FASDs and adoption, particularly where CYP are adopted from abroad, Del Campo (2010) explains that providing accurate information to families about the child and their family background is crucial. However, this is often not a priority for private and governmental adoption agencies. In addition, these agencies are not always aware of FASDs as a possible diagnosis, often attributing developmental delays and health problems to early neglect, abuse, institutionalisation, or lack of sensitive parenting. If identification of severe problems occurs only when the child is placed in an adoptive family, this can lead to 'problems and dysfunction in the adoptive family', possibly resulting in 'rejection of the CYP or other major problems' (ibid., p. 55). It is important not to make ethical judgements about families if this happens. Table 6.1 summarises these issues pragmatically.

An increasing number of CYP are being adopted from abroad (Rampage et al., 2003), particularly from countries where there has been social upheaval or dire economic circumstances resulting in many children being placed in orphanages and institutional care. This can pose issues for increased attachment difficulties, and, if the child has a different ethnic or racial

Table 6.1 Ethical considerations relating to adoption

Adoption facts	Adoption outcomes
Many parents want a healthy child	Not all children are healthy
Parenting child CYP with a disability is different	Not all parents can deal with a disability
Adoption is a difficult (obscure) process	Access to information is poor
Adoption is full of feelings	Feelings interfere with fair decisions
Adoption is irreversible	Adoption can be a failure
The happiness of the whole family is at stake	Families suffer

Source: Adapted from Del Campo, 2010.

background from the adoptive parents, the physical dissimilarity among family members means that the adoption will be more public and open to interpretation from others (ibid., p. 211).

Sibling relationships

Relationships amongst siblings in any family often leave parents feeling like intermediaries or referees. In some cases CYP with FASDs are adopted into a family with their natural siblings (who may or may not also have a diagnosis of FASD), and in other cases they will be meeting new siblings when they are placed in a new home.

Children and young people with FASDs can make family life demanding as their challenging behaviour requires predictability and consistency of routine to reduce anxiety, and their demands for attention and need for constant supervision to keep them and others safe can be difficult for siblings to accommodate. One sibling, whose adoptive brother came into her family when she was aged 11 and he was 18 months old, talks about the challenges of living with her brother and the impact on her everyday life:

> I resented my brother. He wound me up, and I could see it destroying the family. Everything always revolved around him. If something good would happen to me, it would quickly be replaced by him doing something bad. Even when he wasn't there, my parents would always be talking about him, and he would dominate any situation. Sounds very petty, but even at my wedding and the birth of my first child he managed to upset my parents and cause chaos.
>
> (Anonymous sibling, personal communication, 2009)

Rampage and colleagues (2003) explain that siblings already in the adoptive family can feel 'both an internal sense of privilege and unconscious guilt in the face of their entitlement' and may begin to wonder about the circumstances of the sibling's birth and develop uncertainty about their own origins (p. 215). If an adoptive child arrives within a new family without his/her natural siblings, the attachment they may feel to their natural siblings and their need to maintain contact with them must not be underestimated, as 'some of the strongest, most positive attachments that CYP coming through the child welfare system have experienced are to siblings' (ibid., p. 215) and these feelings of strong bonds, dependence, and loyalty should be encouraged to ensure emotional well being for the adoptive child.

Supporting and empowering families

Fetal alcohol spectrum disorders are often under-recognised and underdiagnosed (see Chapter 1). Little is known at the present time about FASDs within the education, health, and social care services in the UK. This can have implications for the availability of services offered to families affected by FASDs. Families often refer to the 'battle' they had to endure to receive the support, services, and diagnosis that their son or daughter needed (Whitehurst, 2010), or highlight the lack of knowledge available within statutory services to facilitate access to services (Blackburn, 2010). This can leave families feeling isolated and concerned about their child's future, as evidenced by the comments below (Blackburn, 2010, pp. 29–30):

> I am surprised to have come across so many people who have no awareness of it (FASD), didn't seem to understand the impact it has on all aspects of children's development, but particularly on the way that they learn. We have talked to Educational Psychologists and they've often said that we probably know more than them and sometimes that's a little bit worrying.

> We know our child and we know bits about schools. We assumed that there would be people who knew about people in our child's situation and which school would be best, which would give us a clearer idea about it. It's a difficult decision and we need first hand experience to draw on.

> I'm a bit apprehensive, not sure how he's going to manage and obviously there are certain restrictions he has with having to have 1:1 support . . . there are certain grand ideas he has and things he'd like to do, some of them are totally unrealistic.

> It's that sort of sickening feeling about what's going to happen next that I get.

Children and young people with FASDs will often present with a different set of needs in school from at home and families may have many concerns about how their child will manage through the school day. These concerns should always be taken seriously as it is important that families feel that they have been listened to and their concerns addressed. It is important that CYP with FASDs receive consistency of approach and language in both the home and the school setting as this will help them to make sense of the world and reduce the number of things they need to remember.

Transition from primary to secondary education can be particularly difficult for CYP with FASDs and needs to be carefully managed, to ensure that communication is efficient and services to families do not become disrupted. A full assessment of the child's needs should be undertaken at this time. For teenagers, issues around emotions, friendships and sexual behaviour, independence, and achievement can compound their difficulties. A lack of understanding of the child's particular learning needs can lead to unrealistic expectations. Without sensitive support and communication between primary and secondary schools and families, CYP may experience behavioural, cognitive, and psychological secondary disabilities, for example depression, self harm, loneliness, and low self esteem, leading to disrupted schooling and trouble with the law. Furthermore, this is a particularly worrying time for families and they will need additional support from schools and supporting services to ensure a smooth transition.

Educators can best support and empower families by providing information relating to the services available to them, sharing information with families relating to classroom activities and curricula, listening to and understanding their concerns relating to their child, and providing an empathetic, non-judgemental culture within the school environment where families feel safe and secure in sharing their concerns, successes, and endeavours to achieve the best outcomes for their son or daughter.

Note

1 The Strange Situation was designed to assess how well an infant uses the caregiver as a secure base for exploration, and is comforted by the caregiver after a mildly stressful experience, such as the mother leaving and then reuniting with the infant. Infants are judged to have a 'secure' attachment if they explore the Strange Situation room and act friendly before the separation from the caregiver, show mild wariness to a stranger during the separation, and are comforted and do not show anger when reunited with the caregiver (Rogoff, 2003).

References

Ainsworth, M.D.S., Biehar, M.C., Waters, E., and Wall, S. (1978) *Patterns of Attachment: A Psychological Study of the Strange Situation.* Hillsdale, NJ: Earlbaum.

Astley, S.J., Stachowiak, J., Clarren, S.K., and Clausen, C. (2002) 'Application of the fetal alcohol syndrome facial photographic screening tool in a foster care population', *Journal of Pediatrics*, 141 (5): 712–717.

Blackburn, C. (2010) *Facing the Challenge and Shaping the Future for Primary and Secondary Aged Students with Foetal Alcohol Spectrum Disorders* (FAS-eD Project). London: National Organisation on Fetal Alcohol Syndrome (UK).

Blackburn, C. (2008) 'What support and advice do parents need following diagnosis of their young child's known or emerging disability/illness?'. Unpublished report for the Children's Workforce Development Council Practitioner Led Research Projects 2007–2008/Pre-School Learning Alliance: Bromsgrove (available on request from carolynb@fasdeducation.org.uk).

Bowlby, J. (1969) *Attachment and Loss. Vol. 1: Attachment.* London: Holgarth Press.

Carpenter, B. (2005) 'Real prospects for early childhood intervention family aspirations and professional implications', in Carpenter, B. and Egerton, J. (eds) *Early Childhood Intervention International Perspectives,*

National Initiatives and Regional Practice. Coventry: West Midlands SEN Regional Partnership, pp. 13–38.

Carpenter, B. and Egerton, J. (2006) Family Structures. Working in Partnership through Early Support: Distance Learning Text. London: Department for Education and Skills.

Davies, J. (2005) 'First impressions: emotional and practical support for families of a child with a learning disability', in Carpenter, B. and Egerton, J. (eds) (2005) *Early Childhood Intervention International Perspectives, National Initiatives and Regional Practice.* Coventry: West Midlands SEN Regional Partnership, pp. 97–106.

Del Campo, M. (2010) 'FASD and adoption: ethical issues'. Parallel Session, First European Conference on FASD, Holland (3–5 November).

Foundation for People with Learning Disabilities (FPLD) (2005) *First Impressions: Emotional and Practical Support for Families of a Young Child with a Learning Disability: A Guide for Practitioners and Service Commissioners.* London: Mental Health Foundation.

Kearney, P. and Griffin, T. (2001) 'Between joy and sorrow: being a parent of a child with developmental disability', *Journal of Advanced Nursing,* 34 (5): 582–592.

McConkey, R., Barr, O., and Baxter, R. (2007) *Complex Needs: The Nursing Response to Children and Young People with Complex Physical Healthcare Need.* Belfast: Institute of Nursing Research, University of Ulster/Department of Health.

Main, M. and Cassidy, J. (1988) 'Categories of response to reunion with the parent at age 6: predictable from infant attachment classifications and stable over a 1-month period', *Developmental Psychology,* 24: 415–426.

Main, M. and Solomon, J. (1986) 'Procedures for identifying infants as disorganised/disorientated during the strange situation', in Greenberg, M.T., Cicchetti, D., and Cummings, E.M (eds) *Attachment in the Pre-School Years: Theory, Research and Intervention.* Chicago: University of Chicago Press, pp. 121–160.

May, P.A., Fiorentino, D., Gossage, P.J., Kalberg, W.O., Hoyme, E.H., Robinson, L.K., Coriale, G., Jones, K.L., del Campo, M., Tarani, L., Romeo, M., Kodituwakku, P.W., Deiana, L., Buckley, D., and Ceccanti, M. (2006) 'Epidemiology of FASD in a province in Italy: prevalence and characteristics of children in a random sample of schools', *Alcoholism: Clinical and Experimental Research,* 30 (9): 1562–1575.

Miyake, K., Chen, S.J., and Campos, J.J. (1985) 'Infant temperament, mother's mode of interaction, and attachment in Japan: an interim report', in Bretherton, I. and Waters, E. (eds) *Growing Points of Attachment Theory and Research. Monographs of the Society for Research in Child Development,* 50 (1–2 Serial no. 209), p. 276–297.

Rampage, C., Eovaldi, M., Ma, C., and Weigel-Foy, E. (2003) 'Adoptive families', in Walsh, F. (ed.) *Normal Family Processes: Growing Diversity and Complexity.* New York: Guildford Press, pp. 210–232.

Rogoff, B. (2003) *The Cultural Nature of Human Development.* Oxford: Oxford University Press.

Sergeant, A. (2010) *Working within Child and Adolescent Mental Health Inpatient Services: A Practitioner's Handbook.* Edited by Barrett, C. Wigan: National CAMHS Support Service.

Scheper-Hughes, N. (1985) 'Culture, scarcity, and maternal thinking: maternal detachment and infant survival in a Brazilian shantytown', *Ethos,* 13: 291–317.

Specialist Schools and Academies Trust (2010) *Complex Learning Difficulties and Disabilities Research Project Attachment Information Sheet.* London: Specialist Schools and Academies Trust. Online at: http://complexld.ssatrust.org.uk/project-information.html, accessed 27 January 2012.

Streissguth, A., Clarren, S., and Jones, K. (1985) 'Natural history of the fetal alcohol syndrome: a 10-year follow-up of eleven patients', *Lancet*, 2: 85–91.

Whitehurst, T. (2010) 'Making sense of FASD: parenting a child with Foetal Alcohol Spectrum Disorder' (unpublished thesis for MSc Clinical Neuropyschiatry). Birmingham: University of Birmingham, School of Medicine.

Chapter 7

Towards a brighter future

The role of teachers in building a platform for change in societal perceptions

Developing an appropriate curriculum for children with fetal alcohol spectrum disorders

Children and young people (CYP) with fetal alcohol spectrum disorders (FASDs) have a range of practical strengths, which can be observed and recorded in the context of the school curriculum. However, including CYP with this condition in all aspects of the English National Curriculum within the full range of educational provision available in this country poses challenges for educators as well as opportunities. As Carpenter and colleagues (2011) note, CYP with FASDs are newly acknowledged in the UK as a group of learners needing specialised intervention. CYP with FASDs may range across the learning disability spectrum from mild to profound. Neuroscience shows that, with FASDs, the brain's parietal lobe can be significantly reduced. This area controls numeracy and mathematical computation. However skilled an educator may be in differentiating the maths curriculum, if that part of the brain is compromised just how do we teach maths to this child (ibid.)?

The complexity of the needs of CYP with FASDs lies not only in the range of learning difficulties highlighted in the pages of this publication but also in other compounding factors such as overlapping and co-morbid conditions, personal family history (which may involve multiple foster and/or adoptive placements), a lack of ability to acquire basic life skills, difficulty in interacting appropriately and on an equal basis with peers, the potential isolation and loneliness born from being the only student in a school with the condition, lack of knowledge about the condition within the education, health, and social care systems and society in general, and the hidden nature of their difficulties. This makes these CYP particularly vulnerable at all ages and stages of the education system and in life generally, and this is certainly a concern shared by parents and educators alike.

Lack of knowledge about CYP with complex needs and the implications for inclusive practice are highlighted in the Salt Review (DCSF, 2010):

> Anecdotal evidence suggests that the increasingly complex needs of SLD/PMLD [Severe Learning Difficulties/Profound and Multiple Learning Difficulties] pupils are not always understood and therefore not always being met.
>
> (p. 3)

There is much for educators to learn about the neuropsychological aspects of FASDs. This is important, as an understanding of 'neurodiversity' in the classroom (McPhillips *et al.*, 2010), where educators have an increased awareness of the scientific basis of biological diversity and how it relates to the needs of their CYP, invites schools to personalise learning (ibid.). This can only improve the school experience for CYP with FASDs.

Parents and educators state that important teaching and learning strategies/environments for CYP with FASDs include small class sizes, high adult to child ratios, adaptation of the physical environment, and the use of concrete visual resources to support teaching and learning (Blackburn, 2010; Carpenter, 2011). This is an area where future educational studies could usefully investigate the effectiveness of interventions and strategies to increase students' motivation and engagement levels in order to improve their life chances. These may include therapeutic, as well as academic, approaches aimed at improving working memory, organisation skills, peer relationships, social and emotional development, and resilience.

Children and young people with FASDs can seem able and to be working at an appropriate curriculum level for their age (Blackburn, 2010). Indeed, in some special school classrooms, educators have commented that the child with an FASD was amongst the most able in the classroom (ibid.). This does not necessarily reflect their skills in other areas, however:

> That's where children like David fall down. He seems like he's doing well and he's got it sussed. He sounds like a capable student, but he can't separate fact from fantasy. He lives in a world of Disney and make believe. He really believes he can be a superhero, and his understanding of fantasy is comparable with that of a 4 year old.
> (Teacher of a child with an FASD, aged 11, quoted in Blackburn, 2010, p. 67)

In addition, needs for this group of students can include complex medical and health needs, making some CYP physically, as well as emotionally, vulnerable. Their social vulnerability is also of paramount concern. O'Malley (2009) advocates the use of vocational tests or adaptive behaviour tests to assess needs for individuals with FASDs in order to:

> bring to the table the plea of FASD being recognised as a social learning disability because intellectual disability is led by IQ tests, but a social learning disability does not need IQ to lead it.

Cooper and Tiknaz (2007) argue that:

> Traditional approaches to curriculum are narrowly defined, and focus on defining what students are capable of doing by the end of certain stages in their school life in cognitive terms. This term is very broad and can be used to refer to a variety of features of the learning process such as perception, attention, information processing, memory, reasoning, problem solving and organisation of thinking. These elements of human learning do

not represent a comprehensive account of this area and what is missing is an appropriate emphasis on social and emotional dimensions.

(p. 30)

These CYP need a curriculum that will capitalise on their practical skills to strengthen their social and emotional development and their ability to consolidate new memories or connect new knowledge with existing understanding (central to the process of cognitive development; Cooper and Tiknaz 2007). This would fulfil what Bruner and Haste (1987) describe as 'calibration', whereby educators adjust their patterns of engagement with children according to their assessment of students' performance characteristics.

The recent research undertaken by the Department for Education (DfE)-funded Complex Learning Difficulties and Disabilities (CLDD) Research Project explored the concept of engagement extensively (Carpenter et al., 2011). It also discussed the process of curriculum calibration and the process of balancing the curriculum in a responsive, meaningful way to ensure that CYP's learning needs are appropriately met (Carpenter, 2010). Equally important is the process of 'pedagogical reconciliation' (Carpenter et al., 2011), the blending of teaching processes around the child's profile of individual needs. This is particularly pertinent as we endeavour to ensure that our teaching touches CYP with FASDs at their point of learning need. As described earlier, a child with an FASD often has a 'spiky' profile of learning. Hence one area of that profile may dominate (for example, hyperactivity) and the child is taught with approaches suitable for attention deficit hyperactivity disorder (ADHD). This may involve considerable auditory input, reminding the child of 'golden rules' or a behaviour management contract/plan. In reality, the child with an FASD is probably a visually dominant learner, and needs visual clues if they are to have any possibility of self regulating their behaviour.

Further, this type of 'diagnostic overshadowing' can lead to medical interventions (e.g. the administration of Ritalin) that may be unsuitable for CYP with FASDs, as evidenced by one parent's report of her teenage daughter's situation:

> My daughter was diagnosed with ADHD, when in fact a later, more accurate diagnosis revealed FASD. She was prescribed with Ritalin, which at the age of 14, caused psychotic episodes. She became a school refuser, and at 16 years old would not leave her bedroom. From having a wide circle of friends, she was reduced to internet relationships with a resulting lack of self esteem and significant loss of personal ambition.
>
> (Anonymous parent, personal communication, 2011)

Thus, with curriculum calibration the child's profile of need is critically reviewed, in order for a personalised curriculum experience to be designed to match each strand of their learning need. The challenge of this should not be underestimated. A significant shift in thinking alongside an inquiry-based style of teaching would seem to be the way forward (Carpenter, 2010).

Involving therapists as key players within a therapeutic curriculum would be a valuable step forward. However, such services are often in demand and it is not uncommon for schools to be allocated a quota of hours for a therapist, necessitating prioritisation of those children who present the greatest need or challenge. This supports a reactive, rather than a proactive, approach to providing appropriate services for CYP who need them, to their educational detriment. Whereas the complex needs of CYP with FASDs do always manifest themselves behaviourally, some CYP with FASDs, whose behaviour has a lesser impact on their peers, may be overlooked, as this Special Educational Needs Co-ordinator (SENCo) suggested:

> The difference between Molly [student with an FASD] and students with ADHD or ASD is that Molly is no trouble to anyone but herself. She doesn't present a challenge or difficulty to other students.
>
> (Blackburn, 2010, p. 70)

A range of professionals is likely to be involved in the assessment of needs and resulting support package offered to CYP with FASDs. The necessity for ongoing multi-disciplinary assessment of needs, in order to ameliorate the potential for further difficulties that develop as children and young people mature, is clear. Educators have the responsibility for utilising this advice and support in the classroom to optimise engagement and learning opportunities for CYP.

Educators can also help to inform their schools and society about the hidden nature of FASD and the support needs of affected CYP and their families. By working with other educators and therapists in school, and employment agencies, potential employers, respite centres, charities, and other professionals, they can build greater understanding about the vulnerability of both CYP with FASDs and their families, and the need for additional support, partnership, and the personalisation of services.

Fetal alcohol spectrum disorders are the most common non-genetic cause of learning difficulties. More evidence-based teacher research is required into this area of special educational needs (SEN), and there needs to be further investment in investigating how professionals, educational policy, and educational reform can support CYP with FASDs. Carpenter (2010) observes:

> There's a lot of learning to be done. We just need to be open to that . . . and, as a consequence . . . there will be system reform, system development, all of which will lead to better schools and greater engagement of children with Foetal Alcohol Spectrum Disorders.
>
> (p. 72)

We will also need to be mindful about hearing the voices of the children themselves. CYP with FASDs have ambitions for their future and views about their education that they are happy to express in terms of what does and does not work in the classroom for them, and what they would like to be in future years. They also often recognise the best learning style for themselves (visual–kinaesthetic; see Chapter 5), which is not always in line with an educator's preferred auditory–vocal teaching style. As one student interviewed (Carpenter, 2011) stated in recognition of her own visually dominant style of learning:

Show me, don't tell me.

(p. 3)

Curriculum, whatever its basis and nature, must be built around those aspirations if we are to engage CYP with FASDs in learning and improving outcomes for them, ensuring opportunities for success.

References

Blackburn, C. (2010) *Facing the Challenge and Shaping the Future for Primary and Secondary Aged Students with Foetal Alcohol Spectrum Disorders* (FAS-eD Project). London: National Organisation on Fetal Alcohol Syndrome (UK). Online at: www.nofas-uk.org, accessed 27 July 2011.

Bruner, J. and Haste, H. (1987) *Making Sense: The Child's Construction of the World*. London: Methuen.

Carpenter B. (2010) *Interview with Carolyn Blackburn*. Transcript available on request from: carolyn.blackburn@mail.bcu.ac.uk. This interview is also available as a podcast at www.nofus.org. Available online at http://nofasaa1.miniserver.com/~martin/Educational_implications_of_FASD.html, accessed 18 February 2012.

Carpenter, B. (2011) 'Pedagogically bereft! Improving learning outcomes for children with Foetal Alcohol Spectrum Disorders', *British Journal of Special Education*, 38 (1): 37–43.

Carpenter, B., Egerton, J., Brooks, T., Cockbill, B., Fotheringham, J., and Rawson, H. (2011) *The Complex Learning Difficulties and Disabilities Research Project: Developing Meaningful Pathways to Personalised Learning Final Report*. London: Specialist Schools and Academies Trust (SSAT).

Carpenter, B. (2010) *Curriculum Reconciliation and Children with Complex Learning Difficulties and Disabilities*. London: SSAT.

Cooper, P. and Tiknaz, Y. (2007) *Nurture Groups in School and at Home: Connecting with Children with Social, Emotional and Behavioural Difficulties*. London: Jessica Kingsley.

DCSF (Department for Schools Children and Families) and DH (Department for Health) (2008) *Aiming High for Disabled Children: Transforming Services for Disabled Children and their Families*. Nottingham: DCSF Publications.

DCSF (2010) *The Salt Review: Independent Review of Teacher Support for Pupils with Severe, Profound and Multiple Learning Difficulties*. Nottingham: DCSF Publications.

McPhillips, T., Bell, S., and Doveston, M. (2010) 'Overcoming barriers to the acquisition of literacy in twenty-first-century inclusive classrooms', in Rose, R. (ed.) *Confronting Obstacles to Inclusion: International Responses to Developing Inclusive Education*. Oxon: Routledge, pp. 213–226.

O'Malley, K. (2009) 'FASD and Post Traumatic Stress Disorder (PTSD): Where does one begin and where does one end?' Presentation to the 3rd International FASD Conference: Integrating Research Policy and Promoting Practice Around the World, A Catalyst for Change, UBC Interprofessional Continuing Education, Canada.

Appendix A

Benton Gibbard and colleagues (2003) and Kodituwakku and colleagues (2006) summarise the findings of a wide range of neuropsychological research in relation to the impairments experienced by children and young people with fetal alcohol spectrum disorders, and these are presented in Table A.1.

Table A.1 Summary of the findings of neuropsychological research in relation to the difficulties experienced by CYP with FASD

Possible cognitive impairments	• Impaired auditory learning • Impaired non-verbal intellectual ability • Impaired IQ • Memory function impairment, including visual, short-term, working memory, explicit memory functioning, conscious memory recall • Impaired strategic manipulation of information to improve recall • Impaired initial encoding of information • Visual–motor integration and visual–perceptual deficits, including reading disorders, impaired visual–spatial perception • Slow information processing • Impairment of higher-level receptive and expressive language • Impaired comprehension • Impaired arithmetical reasoning and mathematical skills (e.g. money management and telling time) • Cognitive inflexibility • Poor executive function ('dysexecutive syndrome') • Impaired concept formation • Poor abstract reasoning/metacognition • Impaired ability to plan
Possible behavioural/ emotional difficulties	• Difficulty in focusing attention and maintaining attention in the presence of distractors • Poor impulse control/response inhibition • Disorganisation • Impaired persistence • Perseverative behaviour • Attention deficit hyperactivity disorder (usually earlier onset, inattention subtype; often unresponsive to medication) • Developmental, psychiatric, and medical conditions • Attachment disorder • Post-traumatic stress disorder • Anxiety disorders

Possible social difficulties	• Emotional immaturity (e.g. age-inappropriate emotional interactions and responses)
	• Lack of effective reciprocal social behaviour (leading to alienation from others)
	• Difficulty in understanding the social consequences of behaviour
	• Lack of social perception including difficulties with:
	    • detecting and understanding non-verbal communication/subtle social cues;
	    • understanding another's perspective;
	    • self-reflection; and
	    • insight into own actions

Other possible difficulties	• Gross and fine motor function difficulties • Sensory processing difficulties

References

Benton Gibbard, W., Wass, P., and Clarke, M.E. (2003) 'The neuropsychological implications of prenatal alcohol exposure', *Canadian Child and Adolescent Psychiatry Review*, 12 (3), 72–76.

Kodituwakku, P., Coriale, G., Fiorentino, D., Aragon, A.S., Kalberg, W.O., Buckley, D., Gossage, J.P., Ceccanti, M., and May, P.A. (2006) 'Neurobehavioural characteristics of children with fetal alcohol spectrum disorders in communities from Italy: preliminary results', *Alcoholism: Clinical and Experimental Research*, 30 (9), 15511561.

Appendix B

Table B.1 Locations, functions and dysfunctions of the seven senses

Sense	Visual (sight)	Auditory (hearing)	Tactile (touch)	Gustatory (taste)	Olfactory (smell)	Vestibular (balance)	Proprioceptive (body awareness)
Location	Eyes	Inner ear: stimulated by air/sound waves	Skin: density of cell distribution varies throughout the body. Areas of greatest density include mouth and hands	Chemical receptors in the tongue: closely entwined with the olfactory (smell) system	Chemical receptors in the nasal structure: loosely associated with the gustatory system	Inner ear: stimulated by head movements and input from other senses, especially visual	Muscles and joints: activated by muscle contractions and movement
Function	Provides information about objects and persons. Helps define boundaries as we move through time and space	Provides information about sounds in the environment (loud, soft, high, low, near, far)	Provides information about the environment and object qualities (touch, pressure, texture, hard, soft, sharp, dull, heat, cold, pain)	Provides information about different types of taste (sweet, sour, bitter, salty, spicy)	Provides information about different types of smell (musty, acrid, putrid, flowery, pungent)	Provides information about where our body is in space, and whether or not we or our surroundings are moving	Tells about speed and direction of movement. Provides information about where a certain body part is and how it is moving
Hypersensitivity	Acute vision, e.g. an aversion to bright/fluorescent lights, easily distracted	Acute hearing – noise sensitive – avoids crowds and noisy environments	Touch may be painful, they may pull away	Acute taste – may avoid strong tasting foods	Acute smell – may avoid eating foods with strong smells	Dislikes movement, difficulty walking on uneven surfaces, trip easily, poor gross motor skills	Odd body posturing, poor fine motor skills
Hyposensitivity	Staring at lights, reflections, bright colours, touching all objects in a room	Likes loud noises, create noises, e.g. banging	Do not feel pain/ temperature. Like deep pressure, tight clothes, weighted blankets	Mouth everything	Smell everything	Seek movement such as spinning, swinging, rocking	Difficulty knowing where their bodies are – tendency to bump into things, trip over, appear floppy

Source: Brooks, 2010, p. 42. Adapted from Myles et al., 2001, p. 5 and Bogdashina, 2002.

Glossary

Alcohol   An alcoholic drink contains the substance ethanol.

Alcohol metabolism   The body's process of converting ingested alcohol to other compounds. Metabolism results in some substances becoming more or less toxic than those originally ingested. Metabolism involves a number of processes, one of which is oxidation. Through oxidation, alcohol is detoxified and removed from the blood, preventing the alcohol from accumulating and destroying cells and organs. A minute amount of alcohol escapes metabolism and is excreted unchanged in the breath and in urine. Until all the alcohol consumed has been metabolised, it is distributed throughout the body, affecting the brain and other tissues. Women who have problems metabolising alcohol may be more likely to deliver infants with an FASD.

Alcohol-related birth defect (ARBD)   A child with ARBDs displays specific physical anomalies resulting from confirmed prenatal alcohol exposure. These may include heart, skeletal, vision, hearing, and fine/gross motor problems.

Alcohol-related neurodevelopmental disorder (ARND)   A child with an ARND exhibits central nervous system damage resulting from a confirmed history of prenatal alcohol exposure. This may be demonstrated as learning difficulties, poor impulse control, poor social skills, and problems with memory, attention, and judgement.

Amniotic fluid   The amniotic sac is filled with clear, pale straw-coloured fluid, in which the unborn baby floats and moves. The amniotic fluid helps to cushion the baby from bumps and injury, as well as providing the baby with fluids that they can breathe and swallow. The fluid also maintains a constant temperature for the baby. The amniotic sac starts to form and fill with fluid within days of a woman conceiving. Amniotic fluid is mainly water. From about week 10 onwards, the unborn baby passes tiny amounts of urine into the fluid. The amount of amniotic fluid increases gradually during pregnancy until about week 38, when it reduces slightly until the baby is born.

Amygdala   One of two small, almond-shaped masses of grey matter that are part of the limbic system. They are located deep inside the brain between the temporal lobes of the cerebral hemispheres and are involved in emotions, emotional learning, and memory.

Attachment difficulties   Attachment theory is the study of how we attach to people in the early stages of our development. This has an impact on how we view ourselves and will affect our ability to develop relationships throughout our lives. Attachments and relationships are very important, as they help us to maintain our emotional well being.

Attention deficit hyperactivity disorder   A neurodevelopmental disorder characterised by extreme inattention, hyperactivity and impulsiveness. It is thought to result from a neurological dysfunction affecting various parts of the brain, including an imbalance in certain neurotransmitters, such as dopamine and serotonin.

Autistic spectrum disorder   Autism is a neurodevelopmental disorder, which means that it stems in part from an irregularity in the brain. Autism is also referred to as the autistic spectrum or autistic spectrum disorders (ASDs), to indicate that it covers a range of conditions including Asperger syndrome.

Caudate nucleus, putamen, and globus pallidus   These collectively form the basal ganglia, and are involved in movement control. These highly specialised clusters of cells/nuclei are found within the white matter, beneath the cerebral cortex.

Central nervous system (CNS)   The brain and the spinal cord. These control the activities of the body.

Cerebellum   Part of the brain that is responsible for psychomotor function, the cerebellum co-ordinates sensory input from the inner ear and the muscles to provide accurate control of position and movement. The cerebrum is divided into two hemispheres (left and right), each consisting of four lobes (frontal, parietal, occipital, and temporal). The outer layer of the brain is known as the cerebral cortex or the 'grey matter'. It covers the nuclei deep within the cerebral hemisphere known as the 'white matter'.

Cleft   A separation or split in either the upper lip or the roof of the mouth (palate), or sometimes both. It occurs when separate areas of the face do not join together properly when a baby is developing in the womb. The development of the face and the upper lip takes place during the fifth to ninth week of pregnancy. Cleft lips and palates can occur on their own (non-syndromic) or are sometimes part of a wider series of birth defects (syndromic).

Clinical genetics   A medical specialty concerned with the diagnosis of disorders and birth defects caused by genetic mechanisms and with risk estimation and genetic counselling of family members.

Corpus callosum   The bridge of nerve fibres that connects the left and right hemispheres.

Diagnosis   The process of determining disease status through the study of symptom patterns and the factors responsible for producing them.

Dietitian   A trained health professional who works with people to develop a balanced and nutritious diet that will support and maintain their health.

Educational psychologist   A professional who works with teachers and families to help with the problems encountered by CYP in education, which may involve learning difficulties and social or emotional problems.

Executive function deficits   Often attributed to dysfunction in the frontal lobe of the brain, executive function deficits primarily involve difficulty forming, planning, and carrying out goal-directed activities. Executive functions also include the ability to change behaviours in different situations.

Fetal alcohol spectrum disorders (FASDs)   This umbrella term encompasses the range of possible effects of prenatal exposure to alcohol. These effects may include physical, cognitive, behavioural, and/or learning disabilities with lifelong implications. The term FASD is not intended for use as a clinical diagnosis.

Fetal alcohol syndrome (FAS)   This expression is used to describe a specific identifiable group of children who all share certain characteristics: a specific set of facial features, central nervous system (CNS) dysfunction, and often growth deficiency and a scattering of other birth defects resulting from confirmed maternal alcohol exposure.

Fetus   A developing being, usually from 3 months after conception until birth for humans. Prior to that time, the developing being is typically referred to as an embryo.

General practitioner (GP)   A family doctor who works in the community and is often the first point of contact for families.

Grey matter   Closely packed neuron cell bodies form the grey matter of the brain. The grey matter includes regions of the brain involved in muscle control, sensory perceptions, such as seeing and hearing, memory, emotions, and speech.

Hippocampus   This component of the limbic system is important in the formation of memories and other higher functions.

Key worker/lead professional   The co-ordinator of services for a particular child to ensure that the help offered is what parents find most useful and is organised in the way that best suits the child's needs.

Music therapy   For people who find verbal communication an inadequate form of self expression, music therapy offers a safe, secure space for the release of feelings. Music therapy involves a relationship between the therapist and client in which music becomes a way of promoting change and growth.

Neuron   A nerve cell that is the basic building block of the nervous system. Neurons are similar to other cells in the human body in a number of ways, but there is one key difference between neurons and other cells. Neurons are specialised to transmit information throughout the body. Sensory neurons carry information from the sensory receptor cells throughout the body to the brain. Motor neurons transmit information from the brain to the muscles of the body. Interneurons are responsible for communicating information between different neurons in the body.

Neurodevelopmental disorder   A range of difficulties wherein there are gaps, delays, or variations in the way a child's brain develops. It can be caused by genetic, environmental, or unspecified reasons, many of which are not yet known. These dysfunctions often interfere with learning, behaviour, and adaptability across environments.

Neurotransmitter   A chemical that is released from a nerve cell which thereby transmits an impulse from a nerve cell to another nerve, muscle, organ, or other tissue. A neuro-transmitter is a messenger of nervous information from one cell to another.

Occupational therapist   A trained and registered health professional who uses mental or physical activity to help people to recover from a disease or injury. They help children improve their developmental function by therapeutic techniques and advise on the use of specialist equipment and environmental adaptations.

Oppositional defiant disorder (ODD)   The essential feature of ODD is a recurrent pattern of negative, defiant, disobedient, and hostile behaviour towards authority figures that persists for at least 6 months. Physical aggression is not typically seen in those with ODD. Some individuals with an FASD may be diagnosed with ODD, which could be co-occurring ODD. Others may seem oppositional but may not understand the request made or be able to follow multiple directions. They may be misdiagnosed with ODD.

Orthoptist   A specialist in the correction of vision by non-surgical means.

Paediatrician   A doctor who specialises in working with babies and children.

Partial fetal alcohol syndrome (pFAS)   This condition indicates confirmed maternal alcohol exposure. A child with pFAS exhibits some, but not all, of the physical signs of FAS, and also has learning and behavioural difficulties which imply CNS damage.

Philtrum   The vertical groove between the nose and the middle part of the upper lip. Individuals diagnosed with FAS have a flattening of the philtrum.

Physiotherapist   A trained and registered health professional who treats disease, injury or deformity by physical methods, including manipulation, massage, infrared heat treatment, and exercise, but not by drugs. Children affected by FASDs may need help with underdeveloped muscle tone, hip and shoulder joint problems, gross motor skills, and balance.

Placenta   The organ that allows nutrients and oxygen in the mother's blood to pass to the fetus and metabolic waste and carbon dioxide from the fetus to cross in the other direction. The two blood supplies do not mix. When a mother drinks during pregnancy, the alcohol crosses the placenta to the fetus.

Play therapy   A way of helping children express their feelings and deal with their emotional problems, using play as the main communication tool.

Prevalence   The prevalence of a disorder is the number of instances of the disorder in a given population at a designated time. The prevalence of FASDs is estimated to be at least 10 per 1,000 live births.

Psychiatry   The study of mental disorders and their diagnosis, management, and prevention. Psychiatrists are medical doctors who have qualified in psychiatry. They often combine a broad general caseload alongside an area of special expertise and research.

Psychologist   A trained and registered health professional who treats the human mind with a view to encouraging a healthy mindset and affecting behaviour.

Reactive attachment disorder (RAD)   The essential feature of reactive attachment disorder is markedly disturbed and developmentally inappropriate social relatedness in most contexts that begins before the age of 5, and is associated with grossly pathological care. Children with reactive attachment disorder may be excessively inhibited, hypervigilant, or highly ambivalent in response to caregivers, or may exhibit indiscriminate sociability or a lack of selectivity in the choice of attachment figures. Children with an FASD who are adopted or are in foster care may be diagnosed with RAD; however, whether the disturbed pattern of social relating is due to brain damage or environmental causes remains unknown.

Sensory processing disorders (SPDs)   SPD is an umbrella term to cover a variety of neurological disabilities and relates to the inability to use information received through the senses in order to function smoothly in daily life.

Special Educational Needs Co-ordinator (SENCo)   A teacher who has particular responsibility for ensuring that all children with special educational needs (SEN) are receiving the provision that they need.

Speech and language therapist   A trained and registered health professional who works with people to improve their speech and language. Many children affected by FASDs present with advanced expressive language, but poor receptive skills. They may also need help with turn taking, waiting in queues, holding a conversation, and listening skills. In addition, they may experience oral motor difficulties resulting from cleft palate or palatal dysfunction, which may require the support of a specialist cleft palate unit.

Teratogen   Any substance, such as alcohol, or condition, such as measles, that can cause damage to a fetus, resulting in deformed fetal structures. Alcohol causes birth defects and brain damage, resulting in neurobehavioural problems in exposed offspring.

Transdisciplinary practice   This represents the concept of persons from multiple professional backgrounds and expertise working together towards assisting a child and family to achieve one set of goals and objectives or outcomes.

White matter   Neuronal tissue containing mainly long, myelinated axons is known as white matter, or the diencephalon. Situated between the brainstem and cerebellum, the white matter consists of structures at the core of the brain such as the thalamus and hypothalamus. The nuclei of the white matter are involved in the relay of sensory information from the rest of the body to the cerebral cortex, as well as in the regulation of autonomic (unconscious) functions such as body temperature, heart rate, and blood pressure. Certain nuclei within the white matter are involved in the expression of emotions, the release of hormones from the pituitary gland, and the regulation of food and water intake. These nuclei are generally considered part of the limbic system.

Useful websites

British Adoption and Fostering Association: www.baaf.org.uk/

Complex Learning Difficulties and Disabilities (CLDD) Project Resources: http://complexld.ssatrust.org.uk/

European FASD Network: www.eufasd.org/

European Birth Mother Support Network: www.eurobmsn.org/

FASD Trust: www.fasdtrust.co.uk/

FAS Aware UK: www.fasaware.co.uk/

Fetal Alcohol Syndrome Consultation, Education and Training Services, Inc.: www.fascets.org/

Fetal Alcohol Spectrum Disorders (FASD Clinic), Surrey and Borders NHS Trust: www.sabp.nhs.uk/services/specialist/fetal-alcohol-spectrum-disorder-fasd-clinic/fetal-alcohol-spectrum-disorder-fasd-clinic

National Organisation for Foetal Alcohol Syndrome UK (NOFAS-UK): www.nofas-uk.org/

Russell Family Fetal Alcohol Disorders Association: http://rffada.org/

The Adolescent and Children's Trust (TACT): www.tactcare.org.uk

Index

Notes: As the main subjects of this book are fetal alcohol spectrum disorders and education, these terms are kept to a minimum in the index.